Philosophy of Depression and Kriya Yoga

OrangeBooks Publication

1st Floor, Rajhans Arcade, Mall Road, Kohka, Bhilai, Chhattisgarh 490020

Website: **www.orangebooks.in**

Second Edition, 2026

ISBN: 978-93-7426-213-9

PHILOSOPHY
of
DEPRESSION

AND KRIYA YOGA

SUMAN SARAN SINHA

OrangeBooks Publication
www.orangebooks.in

In Loving Memory

Of My Grandfather

(Late Muralidhar (1880-1956),

Renowned Lawyer and Government Advocate

Author's Note

This edition has been substantially revised and reformatted from the earlier independently published version. Errors in typography, layout, pagination, and cover design have been corrected to improve readability.

Why This Book?

This book is not a medical textbook.

It is a philosophical and spiritual inquiry into depression, loneliness, meaning, consciousness and the transformative potential of Kriya Yoga.

It is written for those who seek understanding beyond symptom management and who wish to investigate the deeper dimensions of human suffering.

Preface

The Search for Resonance

One evening, while watching *The National* TV hosted by Matt Galloway in October 2013, I encountered a report that left me unsettled. The findings, drawn from the National College Health Assessment Survey, revealed that nearly 66% of students at Ontario College of Art and Design University had experienced thoughts of suicide. Approximately 15% had seriously contemplated ending their lives because of depression.

Statistics often pass before us like fleeting headlines. Yet behind every number is a human story—a young individual carrying invisible burdens, silently struggling in classrooms, studios, dormitories, and libraries. These are students at a stage of life traditionally associated with aspiration, creativity, and discovery. And yet, many of them are navigating despair.

The report was not merely news. It was a mirror reflecting a deeper social reality—one that demands not only medical analysis but philosophical reflection.

Depression is frequently described as a "loss"—a loss of interest, a loss of energy, a loss of self. However, from a philosophical perspective, depression can be viewed as an **excess of truth.** It is the moment when the illusions we use to navigate the world—the status, the busyness, the superficial connections—suddenly lose their weight. We are left staring at the raw, unvarnished "Nothingness" that lies beneath.

The reasoning is not intended to replace medical intervention, nor is it a romanticization of suffering. It is an inquiry into the **Existential Function** of the low state. We will explore the idea that depression is a "collapse of the worldly self" that is necessary before the "spiritual self" can emerge.

The modern world treats depression primarily as a malfunction—a chemical glitch to be corrected or a social deviation to be hidden. While the clinical lens provides essential tools for survival, it often overlooks the profound, ancient "Why" that lingers in the silence of a darkened room. This book does not seek to replace the medical; rather, it seeks to honor the experience as a significant, albeit painful, stage of human consciousness.

For many, depression is not merely a loss of happiness, but a loss of *world*. It is the moment the stage lights of society flicker out, leaving the individual alone with the raw, unvarnished reality of existence. In this stillness, the questions we usually drown out with busyness become deafening: *Who am I without my roles? What is the value of effort in an indifferent universe? Why does the heart ache for a home it has never visited?*

This book was not written in a vacuum of academic theory, nor was it born from a life of quiet seclusion. It is the result of four decades navigating the complexities of the modern world—a journey that has taken me through the rigorous logic of courtrooms, the high-stakes strategy of global management consulting for business organizations and heads of state, and active leadership as President and Secretary for various social and cultural organizations. Parallel to this has been my journey along the timeless, silent paths of Yoga and philosophy.

Throughout these years, I have lived in the noise of the world. I have witnessed the relentless pursuit of achievement and the intoxicating glow of recognition. Yet, in the boardrooms of power and centers of professional success, I repeatedly encountered a recurring shadow: a pervasive emptiness in many around me that seemed to grow even as external milestones were met. I began to ask a question I saw reflected in the eyes of countless individuals I mentored: *Why do they feel alone, even when their lives appear full?*

My earlier reflections on the philosophy of happiness and philosophy of Loneliness, led naturally to this inquiry. I realized that for many, happiness is not elusive because it is hard to find, but because of an invisible barrier. That barrier is loneliness—not merely the physical state of being alone, but an existential distance from the self and the world.

As an attorney, I learned the importance of clarity and evidence. As a management consultant, I learned the value of identifying root causes. As a thinker, philosopher, practitioner of Ashtanga Yoga and Kriya Yoga, I learned that the answers to our deepest struggles are rarely found on the surface of life; they are found in the forgotten language of stillness.

In this book, I have attempted to bridge these worlds. You will find a blend of psychological insight, philosophical analysis, and spiritual practice. This work does not promise a quick escape from the discomfort of isolation. Instead, it invites you to walk beside your loneliness, to investigate its depths with honesty and hope, and to recognize it as a doorway to inner transformation.

I wrote this book especially for the seeker who feels unseen in a crowded room, for the professional who wonders why success feels hollow, and for the soul searching for a sense of belonging that the world cannot measure. It is my sincere hope that these reflections provide more than just information; I hope they provide a sense of presence—a companionship that guides you toward your own center.

We live in an age of constant connection, yet we are starving for resonance. Let this work be a bridge back to that resonance. Let us step beyond the mind's captivity together and rediscover the silent companionship that has been waiting within us all along.

We will explore

- **The Metaphysics of Melancholy:** How deep sadness can be a precursor to deep seeing.
- **The Ethics of Endurance:** Why staying, even when meaning is absent, is the ultimate philosophical act.
- **The Spiritual Pivot:** The exact moment where "I am nothing" transforms into "I am part of everything."

We do not seek to romanticize pain, for pain is heavy and exhausting. Instead, we seek to **transmute** it. If depression is the "Dark Night of the Soul," then philosophy is the lantern, and spiritualism is the sunrise that follows.

Welcome to the doorway. It is time to see what lies on the other side.

— ***Suman Saran Sinha***

A Note of Caution: Yoga is the natural and holistic way to balance body, mind and soul. However, if you are suffering from acute psychological or physical ailment of concern then you must obtain medical advice before practicing 21-Day Kriya mentioned in this book.

Contents

Introduction

The Architecture of the Abyss

To speak of depression in a philosophical sense is to step away from the pharmacy and into the cathedral of the mind. We are not here to discuss symptoms; we are here to discuss **significance**.

For the seeker, depression is often the first cracks in the hull of a life built on superficiality. It is the moment when the autopilot of daily existence—the career, the social expectations, the relentless pursuit of more—suddenly loses its power to motivate. When the engine of the ego stalls, we find ourselves drifting in a vast, silent ocean. This silence is what we call depression, but if we listen closely, it is also the first breath of a spiritual awakening.

The Great Deconstruction

Before a new structure can be built, the old one must often be cleared away. Philosophy teaches us that our suffering is frequently tied to our attachments. We suffer because we believe we *are* our thoughts, our failures, or our isolation.

In the early stages of this book, we must acknowledge that depression is a **ruthless philosopher**. It strips away the noise of the world and leaves us with the Signal. It forces an uncomfortable honesty:

- **The Illusion of Permanence:** Depression reminds us that everything we cling to is transient.
- **The Myth of Independence:** It reveals the deep, aching void that occurs when we are disconnected from the Universal Whole.
- **The Weight of Choice:** It highlights the exhaustion of trying to construct a self in a world that feels increasingly hollow.

From Loneliness to Solitude

There is a vital distinction we will explore throughout these pages: the difference between **Loneliness** (the painful gap between oneself and others) and **Solitude** (the peaceful communion between oneself and the Universe).

Loneliness is the philosophy of depression in its rawest form—it is the feeling of being an island. However, as we move toward the doorway to awakening, we begin to see that the island is connected to the seabed, and the seabed is part of the earth. The transition from depression to spiritualism is essentially the realization that **you are not the island; you are the Earth.**

The Purpose of This Inquiry

The goal of these opening remarks is to set a foundational truth: **Your despair is not a dead end; it is a laboratory.** We are going to use the tools of logic, existential inquiry, and ancient wisdom to examine the darkness not as a monster to be feared, but as a map to be read. If you feel like you are at the bottom, remember that the bottom is the only place where the foundation is solid enough to build something that lasts.

"The wound is the place where the Light enters you."

— Rumi

This book is the study of that wound. It is the analytical preparation for the spiritual leap. We will not look away from the pain, but we will refuse to let it have the final word. Instead, we will use it as the very fuel for the awakening that follows.

Chapter - 1
The Shadow on Tender Minds

Inherited Debts and the Fragile Foundation

Depression is rarely a sudden storm; more often, it is a rising tide that began in the quiet tributaries of our childhood. For many, the pall of gloom that defines their adult life is not an original creation, but an inheritance. We enter the world as Tender Minds—highly porous, deeply observant, and biologically wired to absorb the emotional atmosphere of our primary environment.

When that environment is defined by domestic instability, the absence of *Samskara* (right impressions) creates a foundation of sand. In Vedic philosophy, *Samskaras* are the grooves in the mind created by experiences. When a child's early grooves are carved by fear, neglect, or inconsistency, the very architecture of their reality is tilted toward despair before they have even uttered their first full sentence.

Depression Beyond the Diagnosis

Depression is frequently described in clinical language: persistent sadness, loss of interest, changes in appetite or sleep, difficulty concentrating, fatigue, feelings of worthlessness. These definitions are essential. Medical science has given us invaluable frameworks for identifying and treating mental illness. Organizations such as the Canadian Mental Health Association and Mental Health America provide critical support, yet statistics and frameworks alone cannot capture the full human experience of depression. There is a subtle, often invisible dimension—an inner silence, a sense of disconnection, a feeling of estrangement from oneself and the world. Clinical definitions map symptoms, but they cannot fully chart the depths of existential loneliness that often accompany them.

In the modern age, these silent struggles are exacerbated by the pressures of constant connectivity. Social media creates curated realities that amplify comparison, inadequacy, and self-doubt. Academic and professional expectations weigh heavily, shaping identities around performance rather than authentic being. The result is a paradox: we are more connected than ever, yet increasingly isolated.

Understanding depression requires moving beyond statistics and symptom checklists. It requires listening to silence, observing the subtle fractures in daily life, and acknowledging the invisible weight many carries. In doing so, we confront not only a personal or medical challenge but a societal and philosophical one: how do we cultivate spaces—both within and around ourselves—that honor the full spectrum of human experience, including suffering, vulnerability, and quiet despair?

As we delve deeper, we see that this silent crisis is not just a statistical anomaly, nor a fleeting trend; it is a wake-up call embedded in our daily rhythms. Across universities, workplaces, and even in the quiet corners of our homes, people are asking: is there a way to reconnect, to find meaning beyond achievement? As a society, we must recognize that mental health is not a separate issue from the way we live; it is woven into the fabric of our expectations, our values, and our relationships.

The Pall of Gloom: A Domestic Atmosphere

We must investigate the family reasons behind the void. In a home where conflict is chronic, silence is weaponized, or emotional availability is a scarce commodity, a child does not simply witness instability; they *become* it.

The nervous system of a child in an unstable home remains in a state of hyper-vigilance, a biological red alert that never stands down.

Over time, this constant state of alarm exhausts the spirit. What we call depression in adulthood is often the collapse of this long-term hyper-vigilance. The mind, tired of scanning for threats that never cease, finally pulls the shutters closed. This is the shadow on tender minds—a defensive retreat into the grey because the bright colors of life felt too dangerous to navigate during our formative years.

The Philosophy of Inherited Debt

Vedic philosophy speaks of ***Prarabdha Karma***—the portion of our past that we are meant to experience in this life. Often, this includes the emotional debts of our ancestors. If a parent never processed their own grief, they pass that unrendered "grey" onto the child as a baseline reality.

You may find yourself carrying a heavy, inexplicable sorrow that feels decades older than you are. This is the ancestral shadow. Philosophically, we must ask: *Is this pain mine, or am I merely the current vessel for a family's unwept tears?* When we view depression as an inherited debt, it shifts from a personal failure to a historical circumstance.

The Biological Cost of the Watchtower

To understand the fragile foundation, we must look at the cost of building a life atop a watchtower. A child raised in a domestic atmosphere of instability is effectively an intelligence officer in their own home. They learn to read the micro-expressions of a volatile parent; they learn the specific cadence of a footstep that signals a coming storm.

While this makes the tender mind incredibly intuitive, it also prevents the development of a safe core. Without a safe core, the individual grows up believing that the world is inherently hostile. Depression, in this context, is a survival mechanism—a way of playing dead so the predator (the environment) loses interest.

Decoupling: Breaking the Script

This is not your burden to "fix," but it is yours to **decouple**. To awaken, you must first recognize that you are currently paying interest on a debt you did not sign for.

By bringing the light of awareness to these inherited patterns, we begin to strengthen the fragile foundation. We move from being a victim of the family script to being the one who finally closes the book on generations of gloom. Decoupling is the process of saying: *"This sorrow was handed to me, but it does not define the essence of who I am."*

Points for Introspection

To move from the shadow toward the awakening, you may reflect on the followings

1. **Identifying the Atmosphere:** If you were to describe the emotional weather of your childhood home in one word (e.g., Static, Thunderous, Freezing, Foggy), what would it be? How does that weather persist in your mind today?
2. **Locating the Debt:** Think of a recurring negative thought or a specific "grey" feeling. Ask yourself: *Whose voice is this?* Does it sound like yours, or does it echo the unfulfilled anxieties of a parent or grandparent?
3. **Recognizing Hyper-Vigilance:** In your daily life, are you still scanning the shores for threats? List three situations where you feel a biological red alert even when no immediate danger is present.
4. **The Samskara Audit:** What are the grooves in your mind? Identify one foundation of sand (a belief based on childhood instability) and describe what a foundation of stone (a belief based on your present strength) would look like.
5. **The Act of Decoupling:** Write a letter of resignation to your inherited debt. Explicitly state which emotional burdens you are no longer willing to carry for your lineage.

21-Day Kriya: The Earth Seat (Prithvi Sthiti)

This Kriya is specifically designed to provide the stability that was missing in the childhood environment, grounding the nervous system into the Earth.

- **The Physical Seat:** Sit directly on the floor (use a cushion if needed but stay low). This Asana includes standing and sitting both. Here we are talking about sitting pose. Imagine your sit-bones are roots extending deep into the bedrock.
- **The Mudra:** *Prithvi Mudra* (Touch the tip of the ring finger to the tip of the thumb on both hands and keep rest of the fingers straight. Rest both hands on your knees). This mudra increases the earth element within the body, promoting physical and mental strength.
- **The Breathing:** Inhale and Exhale first deeply couple of times then slow down and breath normally while focussing your awareness as above.
- **The 21-Day Progression:**
  - **Days 1–7 (Rooting):** Spend 10 minutes in silence. Focus entirely on the physical sensation of the floor supporting you. Mentally repeat: *"The Earth holds me, even when the world shakes."*
  - **Days 8–14 (Breathing Stability):** Practice *Adham Pranayama* (Abdominal Breathing). As you inhale, feel your belly expand against your lap. As you exhale, feel your weight sink deeper into the floor.
  - **Days 15–21 (The Golden Foundation):** Visualize a golden plate of light beneath you, reinforcing your base. See this light filling the cracks in your foundation caused by past instability.
- **The Goal:** To replace the shaky foundation of childhood with an unshakeable, self-generated sense of safety and belonging.

21-Day Kriya: The Earth Seat
(Prithvi Sthiti)
"The Physical Seat:
Sit-bones are roots
extending deep
into the bedrock."
PRITHVI MUDRA DESCRIPTION
A powerful gesture to connect with the Earth element. By
touching the tip of the ring finger and thumb, it grounding
the body, restores vitality, and balances the Root Chakra
(Muladhara). Best practiced for 15-45 minutes daily.

Chapter - 2
The Myth of Independence

Dharma, Mutual Duty, and the Prison of Isolation

In the contemporary Western paradigm, the ultimate hallmark of maturity is independence. We are conditioned from a young age to strive for a life where we need no one—moving into our own apartments, managing our finances in a vacuum, and solving our emotional crises in a silo of privacy. While this is marketed as the pinnacle of freedom, philosophically and biologically, it is a recipe for catastrophe. We have traded the "Village" for a "Cubicle," and in doing so, we have severed the essential human lines of **Dharma** (mutual duty) that once kept the shadows of depression at bay.

True independence is a myth; interdependence is the reality of the universe. When we look at the cosmos, nothing exists in isolation. The leaf does not claim independence from the branch; the planet does not claim independence from the sun. Yet, the modern human is taught that needing others is a weakness. This myth of independence forces us to carry the heavy burden of existence on two shoulders instead of a thousand, leading to an inevitable collapse of the spirit.

The Critique of Premature Isolation

We must investigate the **Social Reasons** behind the modern epidemic of adolescent and young adult despair. For millennia, the human nervous system co-evolved within the joint family and the communal tribe. In these models, the burden of existence—financial, emotional, and physical—was distributed across a collective. If one member fell into a pall of gloom, there were five others to hold the perimeter.

Today, the push for premature independence has created a society of isolated islands. When you are an island, every storm is a potential shipwreck. This isolation is not freedom; it is a form of sensory and emotional deprivation.

The human brain is literally wired to regulate its emotions through connection with others—a process known as co-regulation. When we isolate prematurely, we lose our external regulators. The phantom pain of depression is often the cry of a social animal that has been separated from its pack. We are experiencing the biological mourning of a connection we were never supposed to lose.

The Cubicle vs. The Commons

The "Cubicle" is not just a workspace; it is a state of mind. It represents the compartmentalization of life. We work in one box, sleep in another, and consume entertainment in a third. In the "Commons" of the traditional village, life was integrated. Your work was your contribution to the tribe; your sorrow was witnessed by the elders; your joy was celebrated by the youth.

In the cubicle existence, our *Dharma* is reduced to a contract. We do a job for a wage, and we pay for services. But you cannot pay for the feeling of being *known*. You cannot outsource the sense of belonging. Depression thrives in the gap between having services and having a community. The modern individual may have 500 digital friends but not a single person who would notice if they didn't emerge from their room for three days. This is the **Prison of Isolation**, where the walls are made of our own desire for autonomy.

Reclaiming the Philosophy of Dharma

To heal, we must move away from the ego's pride of doing it alone and return to the Vedantic concept of ***Dharma***. In this context, *Dharma* is the realization that caring for others, and allowing ourselves to be cared for, is an alignment with the cosmic order.

Dharma is the glue of the universe. It suggests that we are not here to be free from each other, but to be responsible for each other. When we embrace our duty to the collective—whether that is a biological family, a spiritual community, or a chosen tribe—the weight of our personal depression begins to dissipate. Why? Because the focus shifts from the internal "I" to the external "We." In the service of others, the ego's grievances lose their central stage. We dissolve the walls of the prison we accidentally built in our search for freedom.

The Spiritual Pivot: From Island to Ocean

The myth of independence is the final hurdle before spiritual awakening. If you believe you are a separate entity struggling against a cold world, depression will be your constant shadow. The doorway to awakening opens when you realize that your isolation was an optical illusion of the ego.

By re-establishing our place within the village, we don't lose our identity; we find our purpose. We begin to understand that our personal suffering is a signal to reconnect. The pall of gloom is the soul's way of saying: *Come back to the fold. You were never meant to carry this alone.*

***"The purpose of the darkness was never to imprison you.
It was to teach you that the light you seek has always been waiting within."***

— *Suman Saran Sinha*

Points for Introspection

To bridge the gap between your current isolation and the *Dharma* of awakening, reflect on these points

1. **The Autonomy Audit:** In what areas of your life do you take pride in needing no one? Does this independence feel like a source of strength, or does it feel like a heavy, lonely backpack?

2. **Defining Your Village:** If you were to fall into a deep crisis tonight, who are the five people who would hold the perimeter? If that list is short, is it because people aren't there, or because you haven't allowed them to see your vulnerability?

3. **The Phantom Pain of Connection:** Recall a time when you felt truly part of something (a team, a family dinner, a volunteer group). Compare that feeling to your current cubicle state. What specific emotional nutrients are missing?

4. **Dharma as Medicine:** Identify one small act of mutual duty you can perform this week for someone else. Notice if the act of caring for another temporarily lightens the weight of your own internal gloom.

5. **Deconstructing the Self-Made Myth:** List three things you use or enjoy daily that you could not have produced alone (e.g., the electricity in your home, the food on your plate, the books you read). Spend a moment acknowledging the thousands of invisible people you are already interdependent with.

21-Day Kriya: The Connection Breath (Hridaya Kriya)

This Kriya is designed to break the energetic shell of the isolated ego and expand the heart center.

- **The Physical Seat:** Sit comfortably with a straight spine. Place your right hand over your heart and your left hand over your right.
- **The Breath:** Practice *Sama Vritti Pranayama* (Equal Breathing). Inhale for 4 counts, hold for 4 counts, exhale for 4 counts, hold for 4 counts.
- **The 21-Day Progression**
  - **Days 1–7 (Internal Connection):** During the hold after the inhale, feel the warmth of your own hands. Mentally say: *"I am not alone; I am part of the Whole."*
  - **Days 8–14 (Expanding the Circle):** Visualize a loved one or a mentor. Imagine a golden thread connecting your heart to theirs. Inhale their support; exhale your gratitude.
  - **Days 15–21 (The Universal Web):** Visualize a web of light connecting every living being. Feel yourself as a vital knot in that web. Recognize that if you fall, the web catches you.
- **The Goal:** To rewire the brain to perceive support as a natural state rather than a shameful necessity.

21-Day Kriya: The Connection Breath (Hridaya Kriya)

Designed to break the energetic 'shell' of the isolated ego and expand the heart center.

Chapter - 3
The Weight of Uncertainty

Artha, Purpose, and the Financial Existential Crisis

In the modern landscape of the soul, we are haunted by a phantom that our ancestors rarely encountered in such a sterile, mathematical form: the "Education without Surety." We are funneled into a system that demands twenty years of our youth and the totality of our cognitive focus, all for the promise of a stability that no longer exists. This creates a specific, crushing brand of depression—a **Financial Existential Crisis**. It is a state where the individual feels like a gear in a machine that is perpetually grinding yet producing nothing of value for the spirit.

In the Vedic tradition, the pursuit of material prosperity is known as ***Artha***. Unlike modern capitalistic views that see wealth as an end, the philosophy of *Artha* posits that material security is a foundational necessity—but only if it serves ***Dharma*** (your righteous purpose or duty). When these two are severed, the result is a profound psychological weight. We are told to work for the sake of working, to earn for the sake of consuming, but without the grounding force of *Dharma*, *Artha* becomes a hollow pursuit that drains the life-force.

The Disconnected Labor

We must look at the root of this heaviness. When we work jobs that feel meaningless or pursue degrees that offer no "surety" of a future, we are practicing *Artha* without *Dharma*. This is like trying to sail a ship with a heavy anchor but no compass. You are exhausted from the effort of moving, yet you are fundamentally lost.

The weight of uncertainty is the psychological tax we pay for living in a state of constant, low-grade survival terror. We are not depressed because we are lazy; we are depressed because our life-force is being traded for bits in a bank account that do not translate into peace in the heart. This disconnection creates a cognitive dissonance where our daily actions do not align with our internal values, leading to a slow erosion of the self.

Education as a Gamble

The pall of gloom often begins in the classroom. When a student realizes that their hard work does not guarantee a place in the world, the subconscious mind enters a state of "Learned Helplessness." Philosophically, this is the death of ***Sankalpa*** (Willpower). If the correlation between effort and outcome is severed, the mind naturally retreats into the fog of depression to protect itself from further disappointment. We are educating the intellect while starving the soul of its need for material prosperity with purpose.

In this state of learned helplessness, the future is no longer a canvas for creation; it is a source of dread. The student or young professional becomes a functional depressive—someone who can perform the tasks required by the machine but has lost the spark of *Sankalpa* that makes life worth living. This is the stage where the doorway to awakening often looks like a brick wall.

Transmuting Uncertainty into Faith

To overcome the weight of uncertainty, we must redefine our relationship with *Artha*. If the system cannot provide surety, we must find surety within our own *Dharma*. This requires a radical shift: moving from seeking security in the external world to seeking alignment in the internal world.

When your work becomes an expression of your duty—even in small ways—the weight of uncertainty begins to lift. You are no longer gambling with your life-force; you are investing it in your own spiritual growth. This is the first step toward the awakening from loneliness to spiritualism, realizing that while you cannot control the economy, you can control the *intent* behind your labour.

Points for Introspection

To evaluate how the weight of uncertainty is impacting your path to awakening, reflect on the following

1. **The *Artha* Audit:** Look at your current daily tasks (work or study). Ask yourself: "Does this labor serve a purpose higher than mere survival?" If the answer is no, how can you infuse one small element of *Dharma* (service or righteousness) into that task today?

2. **Locating the "Survival Terror":** Close your eyes and scan your body. Where do you feel the weight of uncertainty? Is it a tightness in the chest, a knot in the stomach? Acknowledge this as a physical response to a lack of *Sankalpa* (Willpower).

3. **Deconstructing "Learned Helplessness":** Identify one area of your life where you have stopped trying because it doesn't matter anyway. What would happen if you performed that action tomorrow, not for the outcome, but as a spiritual exercise in *Sankalpa*?

4. **The Gamble of Education:** Reflect on your years of schooling. Did the system teach you how to make a living (*Artha*), or did it teach you how to live (*Dharma*)? Write down three things your soul needs to learn that were never mentioned in a classroom.

5. **Reclaiming *Sankalpa*:** Set one tiny, non-negotiable goal for tomorrow that is purely for your own spiritual or mental well-being. By completing it, you are proving to your subconscious that the link between effort and outcome still exists.

21-Day Kriya: The Abundance Flow (Artha Shuddhi)

This Kriya is designed to shift the nervous system from "Scarcity/Survival Mode" to "Abundance/Purpose Mode."

- **The Physical Seat:** Sit in *Sukhasana* (Easy Pose) or Padmasana with a straight spine. Place your hands in *Kubera Mudra* (join the tips of the thumb, index, and middle fingers of left hand; fold the other two into the palm).
- **The Breath (Surya Bhedana):** Close your left nostril with your ring finger of right hand. Inhale deeply through the right nostril to stoke the solar fire of confidence. Close the right nostril with thumb and exhale slowly through the left.
- **The 21-Day Progression**
    - **Days 1–7:** Practice the breath for 5 minutes. Focus on the *Manipura Chakra* (Solar Plexus) placed in the center of vertebral column behind the naval. Visualize a golden sun rising in your gut, burning away the "grey fog" of financial fear.
    - **Days 8–14:** Add the mental affirmation: *"My worth is Infinite; my needs are met."* Repeat this on every exhale.
    - **Days 15–21:** After the breathing, sit in total silence for 10 minutes. Observe the uncertainty as a cloud passing through a vast, unchanging sky. You are the sky, not the cloud.

21-Day Kriya: The Abundance Flow (Artha Shuddhi)

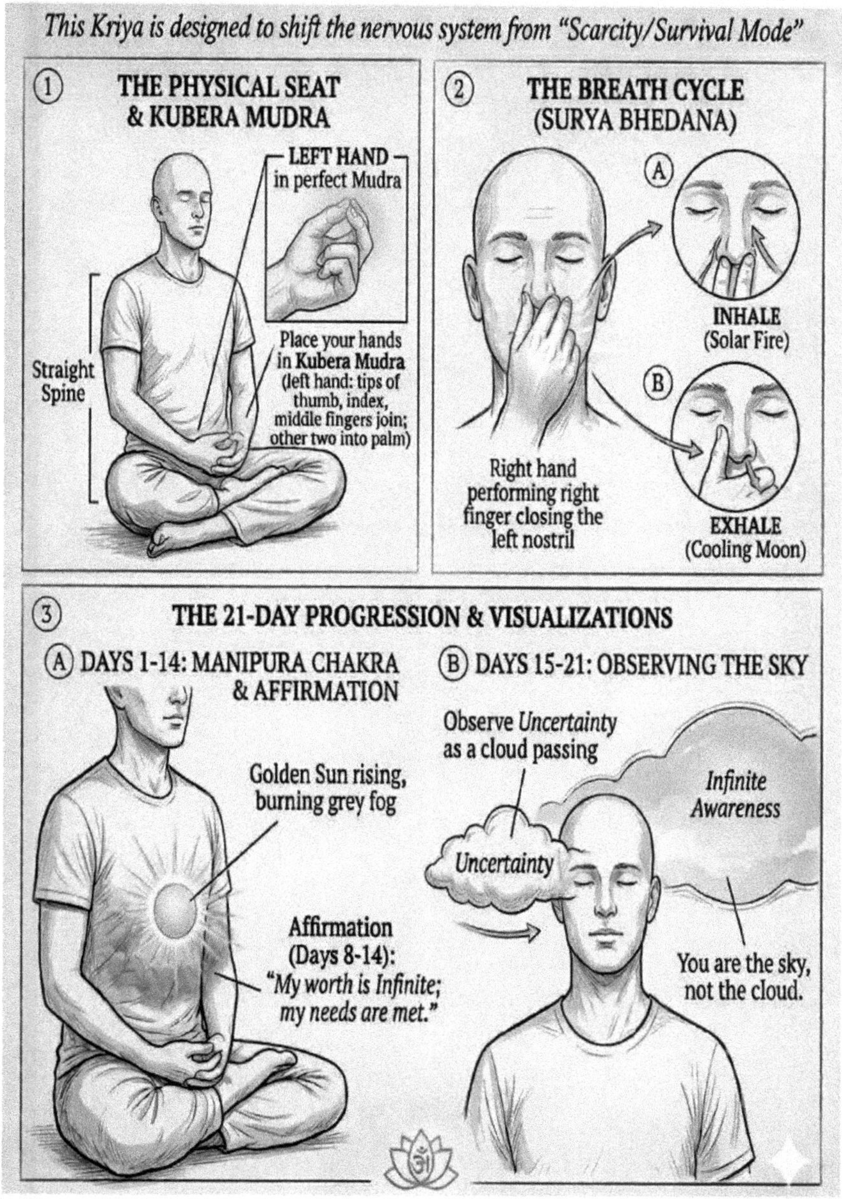

"If depression is the "Dark Night of the Soul," then philosophy is the lantern, and spiritualism is the sunrise that follows."

— Suman Saran Sinha

Chapter - 3 (A)
The Philosophy of Meaning

When Success Feels Empty

One of the great paradoxes of modern civilization is that many people possess more comfort, convenience, and opportunity than any previous generation, yet experience a persistent sense of emptiness. The modern individual may have a stable income, a respectable career, access to entertainment, and a network of acquaintances, but still awaken each morning with a subtle question echoing beneath the routines of daily life: "Is this all there is?"

This question is rarely discussed openly because it is difficult to explain. Society understands hunger, poverty, illness, and failure. It does not easily understand the suffering of a person whose external life appears successful. Yet this form of suffering is increasingly common.

The crisis is not one of possession but of meaning.

For centuries, human beings organized their lives around shared narratives—family, faith, community, service, and a sense of belonging to something larger than themselves. These narratives provided a framework through which suffering could be understood and endured. Modern life has delivered unprecedented freedom, but it has also dismantled many of the structures that once provided meaning.

As a result, many individuals discover that achievement alone cannot answer the deeper questions of existence. A promotion may provide excitement, but not purpose. Recognition may satisfy the ego, but not the soul. Wealth may purchase comfort, but not fulfilment.

The tragedy of meaninglessness is not dramatic. It does not arrive like a storm. It arrives quietly. One continues to work, socialize, and fulfil obligations while feeling increasingly disconnected from one's own life. The days become efficient but not significant. Activity replaces purpose. Motion replaces direction.

From a philosophical perspective, depression often emerges when the individual can no longer ignore this disconnect. The old motivations lose their power, but new ones have not yet appeared. What appears to be psychological collapse may, in some cases, be the beginning of existential inquiry.

The question then changes.

Instead of asking, “How can I become more successful?”

one begins asking,

“Why do I seek success at all?”

This marks the beginning of a different journey—the search not for achievement, but for meaning.

Meaning cannot be purchased, inherited, or imposed from outside. It emerges when one's actions, values, and inner convictions begin to move in the same direction. In Yoga, this alignment is not merely psychological; it is spiritual. It is the gradual movement from fragmentation toward wholeness.

The individual who discovers meaning does not necessarily escape difficulty. Rather, difficulty acquires context. Suffering ceases to be meaningless pain and becomes part of a larger journey of growth, understanding, and transformation.

The absence of meaning creates despair.

The presence of meaning creates endurance.

And endurance, sustained over time, becomes the doorway to awakening.

Chapter - 4
The Ego and the "Ideal Self"

The Philosophy of Hypocrisy and the Digital Mirror

In the modern era, we have transitioned from living our lives to broadcasting them. This shift has birthed a profound existential ailment: the philosophy of hypocrisy. We find ourselves caught in a relentless, silent competition where the "Real Self"—with all its fatigue, doubt, and human messiness—is forced to compete with the "Ideal Self" of others. This ideal self is a curated, polished, and digitally filtered avatar that exists only on screens. The tragedy of our time is that we compare our internal behind-the-scenes footage with everyone else's highlight reel.

This comparison creates a psychic friction that wears down the soul. When we see a peer's curated success, our ego does not see the struggle, the mundane hours, or the hidden failures; it only sees the finished product and judges our own messy process as an inadequacy. We are no longer authentic beings; we are editors of our own existence, constantly trimming away the "unmarketable" parts of our humanity.

The Great Psychic Rift

The ego is naturally designed to seek validation, but social media has hyper-charged this instinct into a predatory loop. When we post a version of our lives that is better than our reality, we create a psychic rift. Every like received for a false persona feels like a hollow victory, because deep down, the soul knows the applause is for the mask, not the wearer. This leads to a unique form of depression: **Performative Exhaustion**. We become tired not from physical labor, but from the immense weight of maintaining a lie.

This exhaustion is cumulative. The more we invest in the ideal self, the more the real self feels like a shameful secret. We begin to loathe the very parts of us that make us human—our vulnerability, our need for rest, and our occasional sadness. This hypocrisy is not just social; it is internal. We develop a "Should-Self"—a list of arbitrary standards of where we should be in life, how we should look, and how happy we should feel. When our authentic experience falls short of this "Should-Self," the ego turns into a prosecutor. Depression, in this context, is the soul's way of going on strike; it is saying: *I will no longer participate in this performance.*

The Commodity of Attention

In the philosophy of hypocrisy, attention becomes the primary currency. However, attention is a poor substitute for connection. We may have thousands of views, but we remain fundamentally lonely because no one is seeing *us*—they are seeing the "Ideal Self" we have projected. This is the ultimate paradox of the digital age: we are more seen than ever before, yet we have never felt more invisible.

The ideal self is a bottomless pit. It requires constant feeding with new content, new achievements, and new validations. This creates a state of pre-emptive anxiety, where we cannot even enjoy a beautiful moment because we are too busy figuring out how to frame it for an audience. We have outsourced our joy to the judgment of strangers.

From Performance to Presence: The Return to Atman

To heal this rift, we must return to the concept of **Atman** (the true, unchanging Self). The Atman does not need an audience. It does not need to be liked, followed, or validated. It simply *is*. The "Ideal Self" is a ghost; it has no substance and can never be satisfied.

By identifying with the **Witness** rather than the **Actor**, we collapse the gap of hypocrisy. We move from a life of impression to a life of expression. Awakening begins when we realize that the "Real Self"—the one that feels pain, the one that is lonely, the one that struggles—is the only self-capable of experiencing true spiritual connection. The mask cannot feel God; only the face can.

Points for Introspection

To bridge the gap between your "Ideal Self" and your "Atman," use these points for deep reflection:

1. **The Mask Audit:** Look through your social media or consider how you present yourself to acquaintances. Identify three things you have shared recently that were curated to look better than they felt. How much energy did it take to maintain that image?
2. **Recognizing the Prosecutor:** For the next 24 hours, listen for the voice of your "Should-Self." Every time you think "I *should* be doing X" or "I *should* feel Y," write it down. Ask yourself: "Whose standard is this? Is it mine, or is it a digital phantom's?"
3. **The Witness Exercise:** When you feel the weight of performative exhaustion," stop and take three deep breaths. Try to step back and simply *watch* the feeling of tiredness. Remind yourself: "I am the one observing the exhaustion; therefore, I am not the exhaustion."
4. **The Joy of the Unseen:** Perform one act of kindness or achieve one small goal this week and tell **no one**. Do not post it, do not mention it in conversation. Notice how it feels to have a secret of the soul that belongs only to you and the Atman.
5. **Deconstructing the Highlight Reel:** The next time you feel less than while looking at someone else's life, consciously remind yourself: "I am comparing my internal reality with their external projection." Imagine what their behind-the-scenes footage might look like at 3:00 AM.
6. **Defining the "Real Self":** List three messy things about yourself that you usually try to hide (e.g., a specific fear, a messy habit, a recurring doubt). Practice saying to yourself: These things do not diminish my worth; they are the terrain upon which my awakening will happen.

21-Day Kriya: The Mirror of Truth (Satya Kriya)

This Kriya focuses on "Pratyahara"—the withdrawal of the senses from external validation—to stabilize the internal self.

- **The Physical Seat:** Sit in front of a mirror in a dimly lit room. Keep the spine erect.
- **The Mudra:** *Hakini Mudra* (place the tips of the fingers of both hands together). This balances the two hemispheres of the brain and integrates the split self.
- **The 21-Day Progression**
  - **Days 1–7 (Observation):** Spend 5 minutes daily in Mirror Meditation, looking at your reflection without judgment. Do not judge the face; just observe the Witness behind the pupils. Inhale Truth, exhale Performance.
  - **Days 8–14 (Cooling):** Add *Sheetali Pranayama* (Cooling Breath). Inhale through a curled tongue (or pursed lips), feeling the cool air hit the back of the throat. This cools the heat of social shame and competition.
  - **Days 15–21 (Affirmation):** While looking in the mirror, say out loud: *"I am the one who sees, not the one who is seen."* Do this for 10 minutes.
- **The Goal:** To break the addiction to external seeing and anchor the consciousness in internal being.

21-Day Kriya: The Mirror of Truth (Satya Kriya)

"The wound may belong to the past,
but the awareness that witnesses it belongs to the eternal."

— Suman Saran Sinha

Chapter - 5
The Silent Witness

The Discovery of the Unshakable Core

Throughout the previous chapters, we have dismantled the weight of being—the inherited debts, the social isolation, the financial anxieties, and the performative exhaustion of the ego. By now, the reader may feel stripped bare, standing in the ruins of their own identity. It is precisely in this state of holy emptiness that we can introduce the most profound concept in the philosophy of the mind: **The Silent Witness** (known in Vedantic tradition as ***Sakshi***).

The fundamental error we make during a depressive episode is one of **identification**. We say, *"I am depressed."* In doing so, we fuse our entire existence with a passing emotional state. However, if you can perceive your depression, then there must be a "perceiver" who is separate from the "thing perceived." If you can observe the pall of gloom rolling in like a fog, you are not the fog; you are the sky that contains it. The sky does not become the fog, even when it is completely obscured by it.

The Observer vs. The Experience

To understand the Silent Witness, we must distinguish between the **Content** of consciousness and the **Container** of consciousness. Depression is content—it is a collection of heavy thoughts, lethargic physical sensations, and grey-toned emotions. The Witness is the container—the vast, silent awareness in which these contents arise, stay for a while, and eventually dissolve.

Think of a movie screen. The screen can show a tragedy, a war, or a dark, lonely room. The screen itself never gets sad. It never catches fire during a scene of a conflagration, and it never gets wet during a storm. It remains white, pristine, and unaffected, regardless of the drama projected upon it. The Silent Witness is your internal screen. Even when the movie of your life feels like a relentless tragedy of isolation, the Witnessing part of you is currently, at this very moment, at peace.

The Part of You That Is Not Depressed

This is a radical claim: **There is a part of you that has never been depressed.**

While your ego is weeping, while your brain chemistry is sluggish, and while your body feels like lead, the Witness is simply observing. It does not judge the depression as bad, nor does it try to fix it. It merely provides the space for the experience to happen. This Witness is the Observer—the part of your consciousness that was there when you were five years old, when you were fifteen, and is there now. It is the unchanging "I" behind the changing "Me."

When we align with the Witness, we begin the process of **Dis-identification**. We move from *"I am sad"* to *"I am aware of a sensation of sadness."* This subtle shift in language is the doorway to awakening. It creates a thin sliver of space—a buffer of light—between the soul and the suffering. In that space, freedom is born.

The Sakshi Bhav: The State of Witnessing

In Eastern philosophy, practicing *Sakshi Bhav* (the attitude of the witness) is the ultimate medicine for the hypocrisy discussed in Chapter 4. The Witness has no ideal self to maintain. It has no need to broadcast its status. It is purely present.

Depression often feels like a closing in on the world—a claustrophobia of the mind. The Witnessing perspective is the antidote because it is inherently expansive. By stepping back into the Observer role, you realize that the depression is just one small weather pattern in the vast climate of your eternal being. You are not a depressed person trying to become a spiritual person. You are a Spiritual Being witnessing a human experience of depression.

The Quiet Power of Non-Resistance

The Witness does not fight the depression. Resistance is the fuel of despair; when we fight our feelings, we give them more power. The Witness, however, practices radical acceptance. It says, *"Ah, so this is what it feels like to feel hopeless today."*

By not resisting, the Witness allows the energy of depression to move through the system more quickly. Depression becomes stuck when we attach stories to it (*"I'll always feel this way," "It's my parents' fault"*). The Witness drops the stories and stays with the raw sensation. In the light of pure, non-judgmental awareness, the pall of gloom begins to lose its density. You are no longer drowning in the ocean; you are the ocean itself, observing its own waves.

"Depression is not always the end of meaning.
Sometimes it is the soul's refusal to live without it."

— *Suman Saran Sinha*

Points for Introspection

To help you locate and strengthen the "Silent Witness" within yourself, contemplate these points

1. **The Language Shift:** For the next hour, every time you feel a heavy emotion, mentally rephrase your thought. Change *"I am tired"* to *"I am aware of a feeling of tiredness."* Change *"I am lonely"* to *"I am observing a sensation of loneliness."* Notice if this creates a small sense of relief or distance.
2. **Locating the Constant:** Think back to a memory from ten years ago. Now, think of a memory from this morning. Is the "Self" that was looking out through your eyes then the same "Self" looking out now? Notice that while your body, thoughts, and circumstances have changed completely, the observer has remained the same.
3. **The Screen and the Movie:** When your mind starts playing a highlight reel of your failures, ask yourself: *"Who is watching this reel?"* Can the viewer be the same as the thing being viewed? If you are the one watching the failure, you cannot *be* the failure.
4. **Scanning for the "Untouched" Space:** Sit quietly and feel the weight of your depression. Now, try to find the edge of that feeling. Is there any part of your awareness—perhaps in the background—that feels neutral or simply still? Focus on that small pocket of stillness. That is the Witness.
5. **Practicing Non-Resistance:** The next time a wave of sadness hits, instead of trying to think your way out of it or distract yourself, say to the feeling: *"You are allowed to be here. I am the space for you."* Observe what happens to the intensity of the feeling when you stop fighting it.
6. **The Witness in the Body:** Close your eyes and observe a physical sensation (like the feeling of your feet on the floor). Notice that the awareness of your feet doesn't have a shape, a weight, or a color. This weightless, shapeless awareness is your true nature. How does it feel to know that your true nature is lighter than your depression?

21-Day Kriya: The Subconscious Reset (Bhramari)

This Kriya uses the state of "Alpha-Theta" brainwaves (the bridge between waking and sleeping) to plant new seeds in the subconscious.

- **The Physical Seat:** Lie in *Savasana* (Corpse Pose) on a flat surface. Cover yourself with a light blanket to maintain body heat.
- **The Mudra:** Keep your palms facing upward, open to receiving.
- **The 21-Day Progression**
  - **Days 1–7 (Clearing):** Practice 5 minutes of *Bhramari Pranayama* (Bee Breath with slow and prolonged humming sound) while lying down. Let the vibration shake loose the mental tension in the skull.
  - **Days 8–14 (Planting the Seed):** After the humming, stay in total stillness. Mentally repeat your *Sankalpa* (a short, positive statement in the present tense, such as *"I am whole and at peace"*) three times with deep feeling.
  - **Days 15–21 (Integration):** Visualize a bright white light at the center of your forehead (the third eye). Imagine this light dissolving the "grey scripts" of your past, leaving a clean, blank slate.
- **The Goal:** To bypass the critical ego-mind and deliver a healing command directly to the subconscious layer where the *Samskara* lives.

21-Day Kriya: The Subconscious Reset (Bhramari)

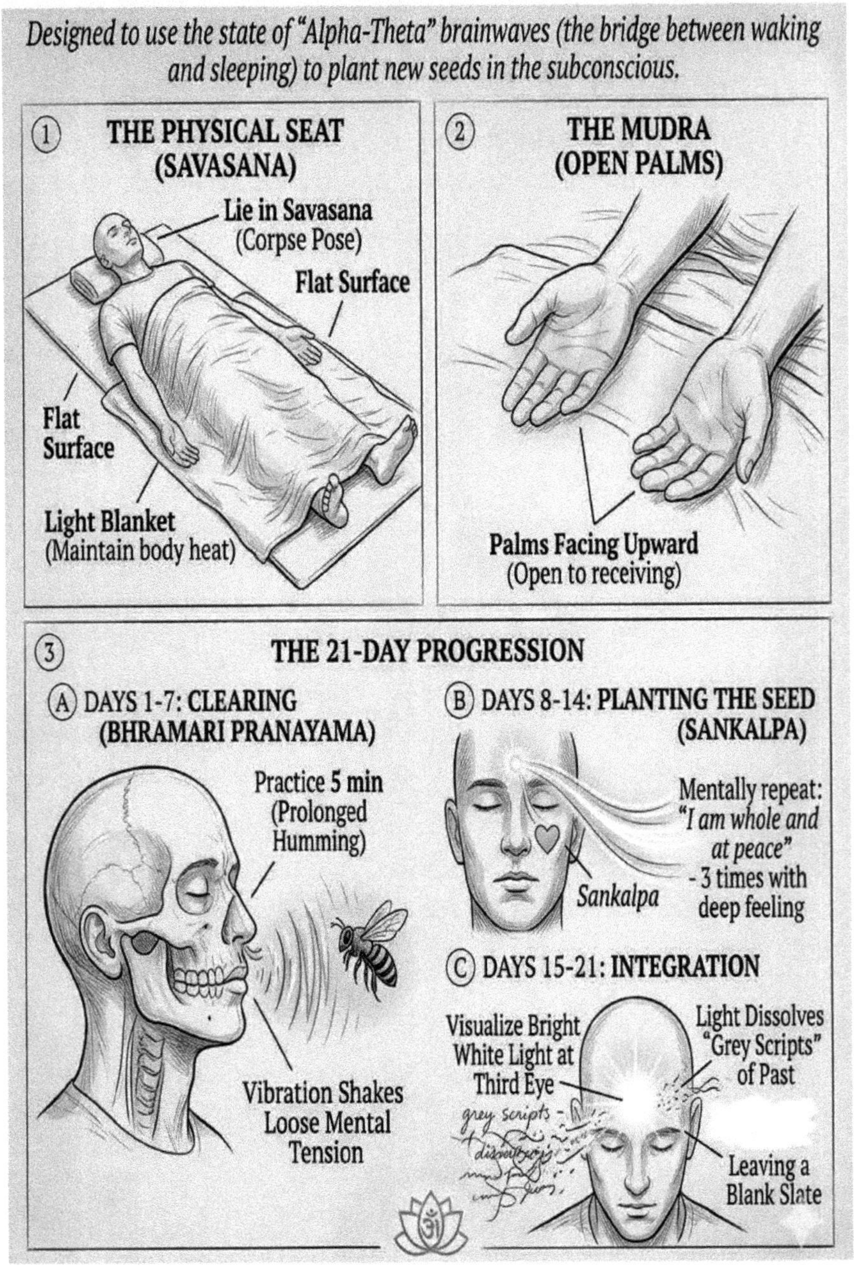

Chapter - 6
The Philosophy of Samskara

Subconscious Software and the Virus of Depression

In the journey from depression to spiritualism, we must eventually descend into the basement of the mind. Philosophically, we are not born as blank slates, nor do we move through life unscathed by our experiences. Every trauma, every harsh word from a parent, and every social failure leaves behind a **Samskara**—a subconscious impression or groove in the mental field. In modern terms, these are the software viruses of the human psyche. When you suffer from chronic depression, you are often not reacting to the present moment; you are running a corrupted script written year, or even decades, ago.

These scripts operate below the level of conscious thought. Just as a computer virus can slow down a system, drain the battery, and cause unexpected crashes without the user seeing the underlying code, *Samskaras* drain our vital energy (***Prana***) and color our reality without our explicit permission. To the depressed mind, the world looks grey not because it *is* grey, but because the lens of the mind is smudged with these old impressions.

The Anatomy of an Impression

A *Samskara* is created when an experience is coupled with a strong emotion. If a child experiences domestic instability (as discussed in Chapter 1), the mind creates a groove of fear and hyper-vigilance. Over time, these grooves become deep canyons. When new life experiences occur, the water of your consciousness naturally flows into these old, deep canyons of despair because it is the path of least resistance.

The philosophy of samskara teaches us that depression is often a mechanical repetition. You are not sad; you are remembering sadness at a cellular level. These impressions act as filters, coloring your perception of the world so that even a sunny day feels grey. To find the doorway to awakening, we must learn the art of ***Chitta Vritti Nirodha***—the stilling of these mental whirlpools—and the conscious rewriting of our internal software.

The Persistence of the Past

Why is it so difficult to just be positive? Because **positivity is a surface-level thought, while a *Samskara* is a structural groove**. A thought is like a leaf floating on the surface of a river; a *Samskara* is the very shape of the riverbed itself. You can throw as many positive leaves as you want into the water, but they will still follow the direction the riverbed dictates.

This explains the relapse nature of depression. An individual might feel better for a few days, but the moment a stressor occurs, the consciousness instinctively falls back into the deep, familiar canyons of the past. The software virus has a self-preservation mechanism: it distorts your logic to make the depression seem realistic and hope seem naive.

Reformatting the Mind: The Power of Sadhana

Rewriting a *Samskara* is not a matter of positive thinking, which is often just a thin coat of paint over a rusted structure. It requires ***Sadhana*** (spiritual discipline) to reach the subconscious depth where the virus resides. By using sound (Mantra), breath (Pranayama), and stillness (Meditation), we create ***Para-Samskaras***—new, powerful, positive impressions that eventually fill the old canyons and redirect the flow of our life force toward peace.

Sadhana is the process of intentional re-grooving. Every time you choose stillness over reaction, every time you choose a mantra over a self-deprecating thought, you are laying a microscopic layer of new sediment in that canyon. Over months and years of consistent practice, the old canyons of despair are filled in, and a new, level plain of consciousness is established. This is the awakening—the moment you realize you are no longer a slave to the corrupted scripts of your childhood.

The Role of the Witness in Rewriting

Recall the **Silent Witness** from Chapter 5. The Witness is the "**System Administrator**" who can see the virus without being infected by it. When you observe a depressive thought arising, you can say, *"That is not me; that is a Samskara running."* This awareness is the anti-virus software. By simply witnessing the groove without flowing into it, you starve the *Samskara* of the emotional energy it needs to grow deeper.

"When every borrowed identity falls away,
what remains is not emptiness—
but the silent presence that was never broken."

— Suman Saran Sinha

Points for Introspection

To begin identifying and reformatting the basement of your mind, reflect on these points

1. **Identifying the "Default Groove":** Think of a small setback you experienced recently (e.g., a critical email, a cancelled plan). What was your *immediate* internal reaction? Was it a reaction to the event itself, or did it feel like a familiar old song playing in your head?
2. **The "Software Virus" Audit:** List three core beliefs you have about yourself when you are depressed (e.g., *"I am a burden," "Nothing ever works out"*). Now, try to trace these back. Can you remember the first time you felt this way as a child? Who helped write this "code?"
3. **Observing the Path of Least Resistance:** Close your eyes and visualize your mind as a landscape of canyons. When you feel a pall of gloom approaching, can you literally feel your thoughts being pulled toward a specific, deep groove of sadness?
4. **The "Thin Coat of Paint" Realization:** Recall a time you tried to think positive but felt like a hypocrite. Acknowledge that you were trying to fix a canyon problem with a leaf solution. How does it feel to realize that you need a deeper, more structural practice (**Sadhana**) rather than just better thoughts?
5. **Selecting Your "Para-Samskara":** Choose a single, powerful word or short phrase (a Mantra) that represents the opposite of your deepest canyon (e.g., *"I am Whole," "I am Peace," "I am Light"*). How would it feel to repeat this word 108 times a day to begin filling that canyon?
6. **The Witness vs. The Virus:** The next time a corrupted script begins to run, mentally say: *"Software update in progress. This script is out of date."* Notice if viewing the depression as a mechanical virus makes it feel less like a personal failure and more like a technical problem to be solved.

21-Day Kriya: The Subconscious Reset (Yoga Nidra Lite)

This Kriya also uses the state of "Alpha-Theta" brainwaves (the bridge between waking and sleeping) to plant new seeds in the subconscious.

- **The Physical Seat:** Lie in *Savasana* (Corpse Pose) on a flat surface. Cover yourself with a light blanket to maintain body heat.
- **The Mudra:** Keep your palms facing upward, open to receiving.
- **The 21-Day Progression**
  - **Days 1–7 (Clearing):** Practice 5 minutes of *Bhramari Pranayama* (Bee Breath) while lying down. Let the vibration shake loose the mental tension in the skull.
  - **Days 8–14 (Planting the Seed):** After the humming, stay in total stillness. Breath slowly and naturally while focusing your awareness on breath. Let all your muscles relax. Mentally repeat your *Sankalpa* (a short, positive statement in the present tense, such as *"I am whole and at peace"*) three times with deep feeling.
  - **Days 15–21 (Integration):** Visualize a bright white light at the center of your forehead (the third eye). Imagine this light dissolving the grey scripts of your past, leaving a clean, blank slate.
- **The Goal:** To bypass the critical ego-mind and deliver a healing command directly to the subconscious layer where the *Samskara* lives.

21-Day Kriya: The Subconscious Reset (Yoga Nidra Lite)

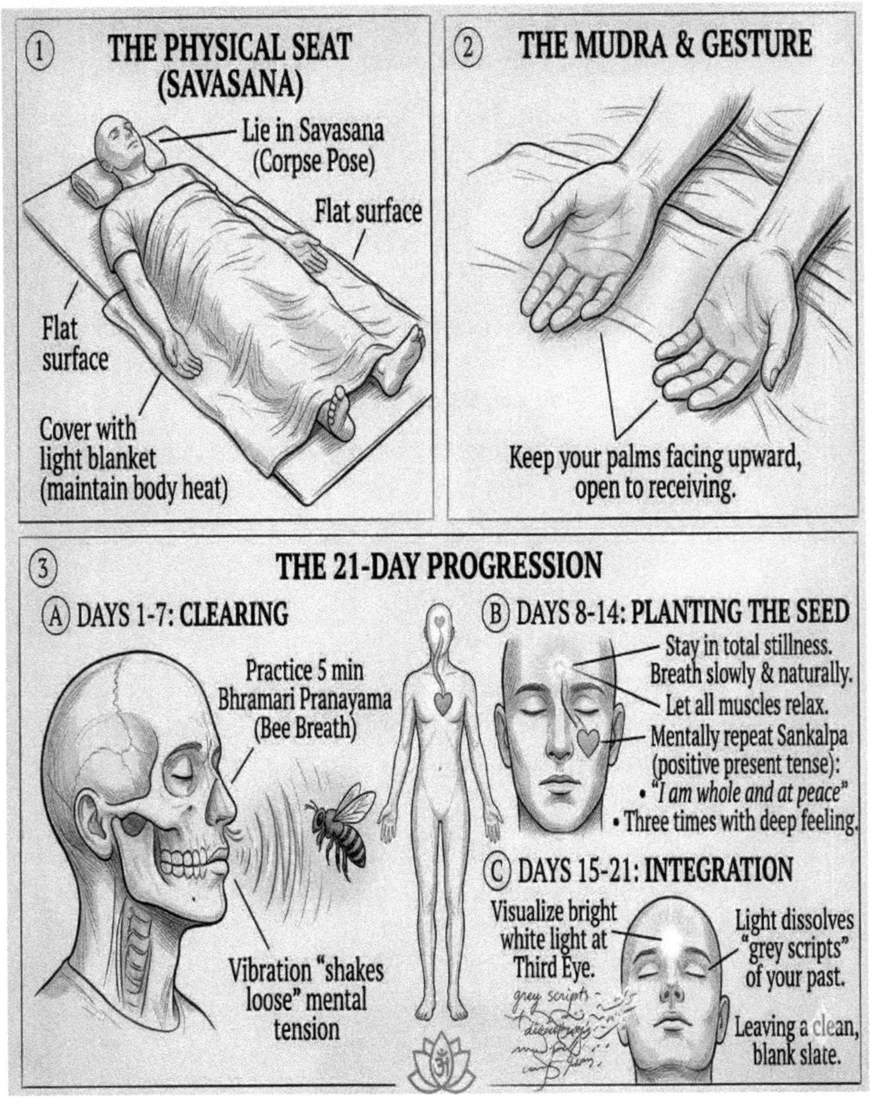

Chapter - 7
The "Pall of Gloom" and Domestic Instability

Investigating Inherited Debts and the Fragile Foundation

If the foundation of a house is cracked, the roof will eventually leak, no matter how much effort is spent polishing the shingles. In this chapter, we investigate the pall of gloom that originates not from our own choices, but from the environment of our early childhood. When a home lacks *Samskara*—the right impressions of safety, stability, and emotional regulation—the child grows up with a nervous system that is perpetually waiting for the other shoe to drop. This chronic state of high alert eventually leads to exhaustion, which the world labels as depression, but which philosophy recognizes as a **Fragile Foundation**.

We must understand that tender minds are highly porous. Just as a plant takes the minerals—or toxins—from the soil in which it is planted, a child absorbs the atmospheric pressure of their home. If that soil is saturated with unexpressed grief or constant conflict, the child's very sense of being becomes inextricably linked to that heaviness. You do not just live in the gloom; you become a biological mirror of it.

The Inherited Emotional Debt

We often carry sadness that does not belong to us. In many families, trauma is passed down like a physical heirloom. A parent's unresolved grief, a grandparent's survival fear, or a household's general pall of gloom becomes the atmospheric pressure in which a tender mind develops. We call this **Inherited Emotional Debt**. You may feel a heavy, unexplained sorrow that is the debt of a previous generation's unexpressed pain.

This debt is often silent. It isn't always found in grand tragedies; it is found in the way a mother sighs when she thinks no one is looking, or the way a father retreats into an icy silence instead of resolving a conflict. As a child, you lacked the philosophical immune system to reject these energies. You accepted the gloom as the "Standard Operating Procedure" for existence. Consequently, as an adult, you may find yourself depressed not because your current life is bad, but because your subconscious is still paying interest on a sorrow that was never yours to begin with.

Ancestral Decoupling: Becoming the Architect

This chapter argues that you are not broken; you are simply holding a weight that was handed to you before you were old enough to refuse it. By identifying these debts, we begin the process of **Ancestral Decoupling**. We realize that while we may have been built on a fragile foundation, we are the architects of the renovation. We move from being a victim of our domestic history to being the one who breaks the cycle.

Decoupling requires the light of awareness. It is the radical act of looking at a feeling of worthlessness and saying: *"This is my father's fear of failure speaking through my vocal cords."* Or looking at a sudden wave of loneliness and recognizing: *"This is the echo of my mother's isolation."* When you name the debt, you stop being the debtor. You begin to see that your "Essential Self" is separate from the "Inherited Shadow."

Reframing the Home as a Temple

To heal, we must consciously create the *Samskaras* that were missing in our youth. We must learn to parent our own inner child with the stability we lacked. This involves a philosophical shift: seeing your current life not as an extension of your past, but as a sovereign territory where you set the emotional laws.

If your first home was a place of instability, your current home—and the home within your own mind—must become a **Temple**. A temple is a space of *Samskara* (right impressions). It is a place where every action is intentional, every word is mindful, and the atmosphere is curated for peace rather than survival. By treating your daily routine as a series of sacred impressions, you slowly replace the fragile foundation with one of solid stone.

Points for Introspection

To begin the renovation of your foundation, reflect on these points of ancestral inquiry

1. **Tracing the Ancestral Fog:** Close your eyes and visualize your parents or the primary caregivers from your childhood. What was the baseline emotion they projected most often? Can you feel that same baseline vibrating in your own chest today?

2. **Identifying the "Inherited Script":** Think of a specific recurring negative thought you have about your future. Does this thought sound like your own adult logic, or does it sound like the survival fear of someone who came before you?

3. **The Architecture of Safety:** List three things that were missing from your childhood home (e.g., laughter, physical affection, calm discussions). How can you intentionally build these into your current environment this week to create a "New Samskara?"

4. **Acknowledging the "Red Alert":** Recall a time today when you felt hyper-vigilant or anxious without an obvious cause. Ask yourself: *"Am I reacting to a present threat, or is my 'Fragile Foundation' just scanning for old ghosts?"*

5. **The Decoupling Declaration:** Write down one specific emotional burden you've carried for years. Now, write a statement of decoupling: *"I acknowledge that this sadness belonged to [Name/Generation], and I gratefully return it to the past. It is not my Dharma to carry it anymore."*

6. **Redefining the Temple:** If your mind is a temple rather than a survival bunker, what is the first impression you want to invite in every morning? Choose one small ritual—a candle, a mantra, or a moment of silence—to serve as a new, solid brick in your foundation.

21-Day Kriya: The Ancestral Release (Pitru Shuddhi)

This Kriya is designed to balance the inherited masculine and feminine energies and release the weight of the past.

- **The Physical Seat:** Sit in a comfortable position with your spine erect. Rest your hands in *Dhyana Mudra* (right hand on top of left, palms up, thumb tips touching), breath slowly with focus on breath.
- **The Breath (Nadi Shodhana):** Alternate Nostril Breathing. After practicing Dhyana Mudra for 5 minutes, Use the right thumb to close the right nostril, inhale deep through the left. Close the left, exhale through the right. Inhale right, exhale left. Repeat 10 or 20 times.
- **The 21-Day Progression**
  - **Days 1–7 (Awareness):** As you breathe through the left nostril (Lunar/Feminine), visualize your maternal line. As you breathe through the right (Solar/Masculine), visualize your paternal line. Simply observe the sensations.
  - **Days 8–14 (Pardon):** During each exhale, mentally whisper: *"I release what is not mine."*
  - Imagine the grey fog of family gloom leaving your body with the breath.
  - **Days 15–21 (The Sovereign Light):** Visualize yourself standing in a circle of white light. See your ancestors standing outside the circle. Bow to them, acknowledging their struggle, but remain firmly within your own light.

21-Day Kriya: The Ancestral Release (Pitru Shuddhi)

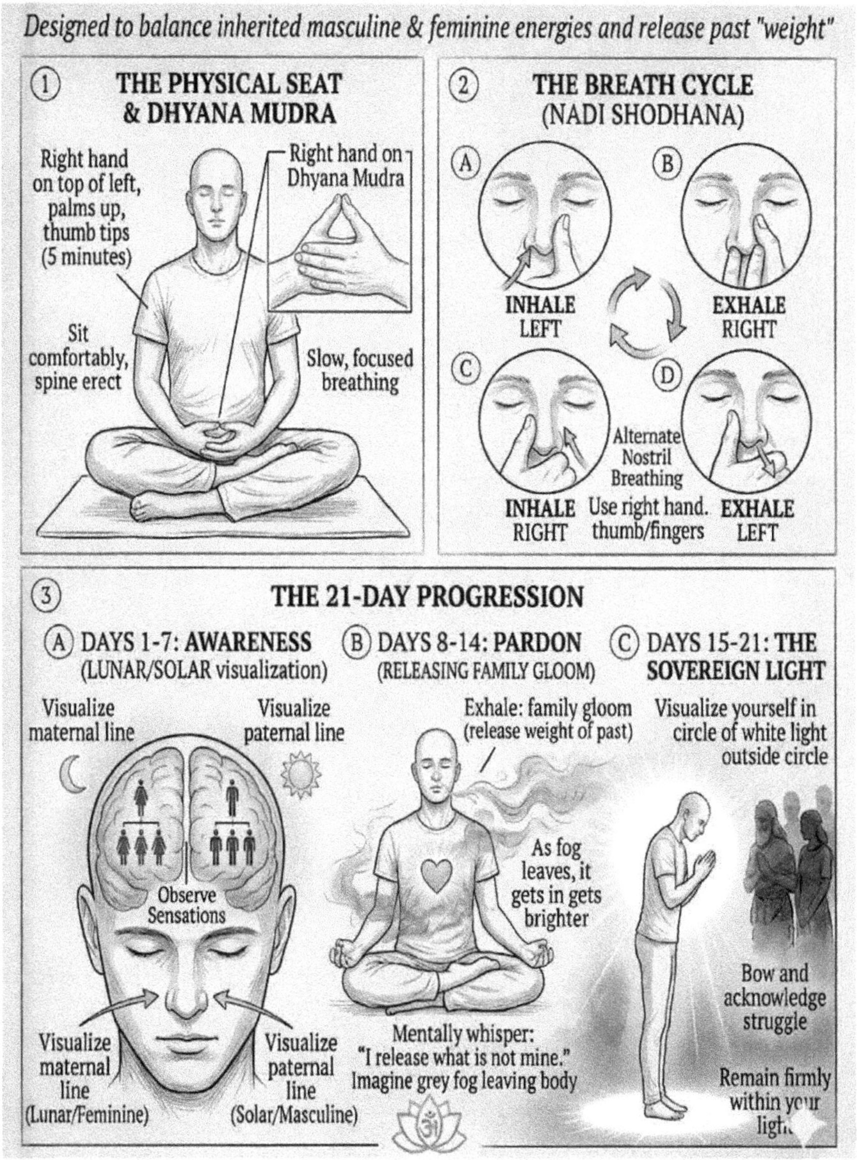

"Dharma is the glue of the universe. It suggests that we are not here to be free from each other, but to be responsible for each other."

— Suman Saran Sinha

Chapter - 8
The Education of the Soul

From Utility to Self-Realization

We live in a society that is highly schooled but largely uneducated in the art of living. From our earliest years, our cognitive development is harnessed for a singular, external purpose: utility. We are taught to calculate, to categorize, and to compete. This is the **Industrial Model of the Mind**, where a human being is viewed as a resource to be optimized for a marketplace. However, when the market fluctuates, or when the job no longer provides a sense of identity, the individual is left in a vacuum. This is the birth of the **Educational Depression**—the realization that you have learned how to make a living, but you have never learned how to *live*.

In this industrial paradigm, depression is often the soul's rebellion against being treated as a tool. When we are reduced to our output, our inner world atrophies. The pall of gloom we feel in adulthood is frequently the exhaustion of a spirit that has been forced to speak the language of efficiency for too long, forgetting its native tongue of meaning.

The Intellectual vs. The Experiential

Modern education prioritizes the accumulation of data over the cultivation of wisdom (*Vidya*). We are taught the history of the world, but not the history of our own patterns. We are taught the laws of physics, but not the laws of our own emotions. This imbalance creates a top-heavy existence. We have giant intellects capable of complex coding or financial modeling, but emotionally, we remain infants, easily toppled by a single wave of loneliness or a moment of uncertainty.

To bridge the gap to spiritualism, we must recognize that true education is experiential, not just informational. You can read a thousand books on peace, but until you experience the silence between two thoughts, you remain uneducated in peace. The **Education of the Soul** requires a re-schooling of our priorities. It is the transition from *Learning for a Career* to *Learning for Character*. In this paradigm, the goal of study is not a degree, but Self-Realization. We begin to treat our internal world with the same rigor and curiosity that we once applied to our textbooks. We move from being informed to being transformed.

The Curriculum of the Inner World

A soul-centered education involves mastering three specific disciplines

1. **Emotional Literacy:** Learning to name and sit with a feeling without being consumed by it.
2. **The Philosophy of Value:** Determining what is "Good" and "True" beyond what is "Profitable."
3. **The Art of Stillness:** Realizing that the most important information does not come from a screen, but from the silence within.

This curriculum is the antidote to the software viruses discussed in Chapter 6. If our early education gave us the viruses of competition and external validation, the Education of the Soul provides the firewall of self-knowledge. We learn that our worth is an inherent quality of our being (*Atman*), not a variable linked to our social or financial performance.

The Graduation from Gloom

The doorway to awakening is essentially a graduation ceremony. It is the moment you stop seeking answers from the systems that made you schooled and start seeking them from the source that makes you wise. When we educate the soul, we stop asking, *what can I get from the world?* and start asking, *what is my true nature?* This shift moves us out of the fragile foundation of societal expectation and onto the solid ground of spiritual identity. We realize that the pall of gloom was not a dead end, but a classroom—a harsh teacher that forced us to look inward when the external world failed to provide lasting satisfaction. By completing the curriculum of the inner world, we find that loneliness was simply the hallway leading us back to the presence of our own divine spark.

"The wound was never the end of the story.
It was the doorway through which awareness entered."

— Suman Saran Sinha

Points for Introspection

To evaluate your own internal schooling and prepare for self-realization, reflect on these points

1. **The Utility Audit:** List three skills you possess that make you useful to the marketplace. Now, list three qualities you possess that make you peaceful within yourself. Which list was easier to write?

2. **Identifying "Top-Heaviness":** Recall a recent moment when you felt emotionally overwhelmed. Did your intellectual knowledge (your degrees, your job skills) help you navigate that emotion, or did you feel like an infant in that moment? What does this tell you about your current educational balance?

3. **The Wisdom (*Vidya*) Gap:** If you were to write a history of your own patterns, what would be the title of the chapter regarding how you handle depression? What recurring lessons have you been forced to repeat?

4. **Defining "The Good":** Aside from money or status, what are three things you consider "True" or "Good?" How much of your weekly schedule is dedicated to these values versus the pursuit of "Utility?"

5. **The Stillness Test:** Sit in absolute silence for five minutes with no phone, music, or books. Observe the "uneducated" part of your mind—the part that gets restless or anxious without external input. What is that restlessness trying to tell you?

6. **Learning for Character:** Identify one emotional pattern you would like to master (e.g., reacting in anger, seeking validation). If you treated this as a major subject in your life's education, what would your daily homework look like?

21-Day Kriya: The Wisdom Eye (Gyana Kriya)

This Kriya is designed to activate the Ajna Chakra (The Third Eye), the seat of intuition and inner knowing, to move beyond intellectual data into direct wisdom.

- **The Physical Seat:** Sit in a meditative posture. Tuck your chin slightly to lengthen the back of the neck.
- **The Mudra:** *Jnana Mudra* (Touch the tip of the index finger to the tip of the thumb, other three fingers extended). Rest them on your knees, palms up.
- **The 21-Day Progression**
    - **Days 1–7 (Internal Focus):** Close your eyes and take your awareness toward the space between your eyebrows. Breathe naturally. Each time a thought about work or chores arises, mentally label it "Information" and return to the "Stillness."
    - **Days 8–14 (The Sound of Wisdom):** While focusing on the third eye, chant the *Bija mantra* **"OM"** slowly. Feel the vibration vibrating in the center of your skull, clearing the cobwebs of useless data.
    - **Days 15–21 (The Questioning):** In the silence after the chant, ask your inner self: *What is the one truth I need to know today?* Do not look for a verbal answer; wait for a feeling or a sense of clarity.
- **The Goal:** To develop a sense of self that is anchored in your own inner authority rather than external validation or academic achievement.

21-Day Kriya: The Wisdom Eye (Gyana Kriya)

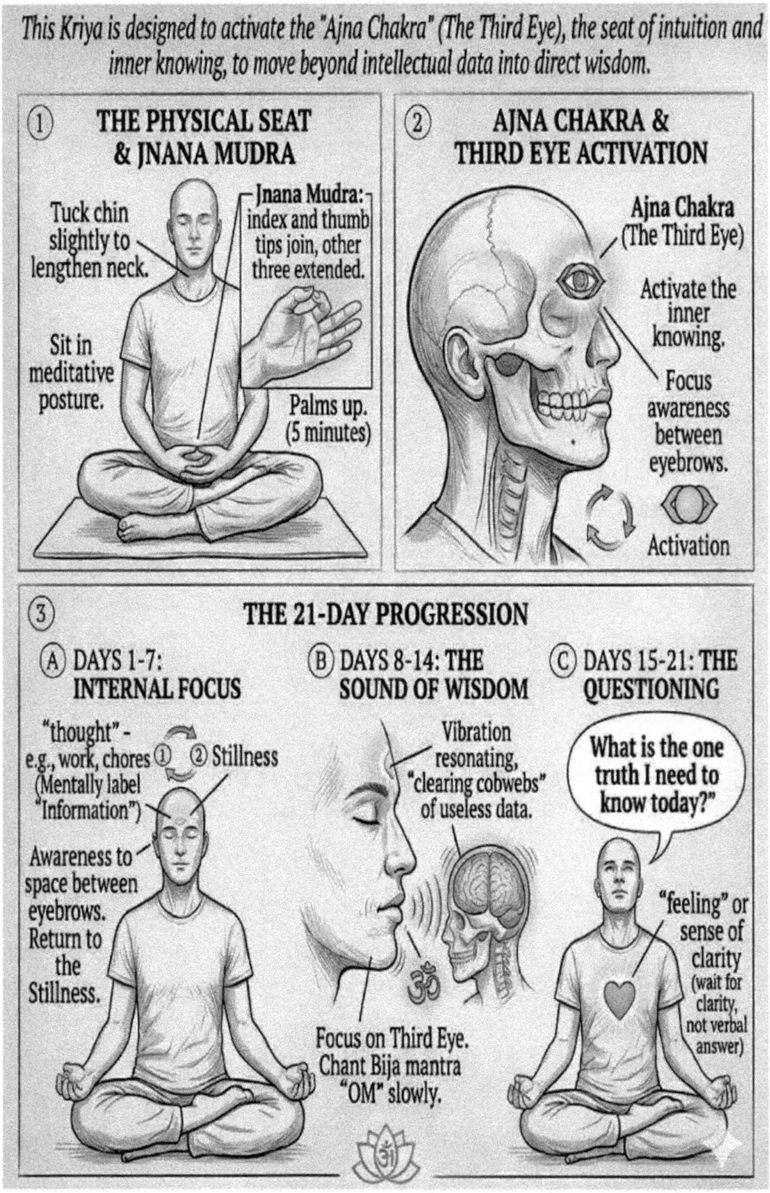

Chapter - 9
Rewriting the Subconscious Script

Sadhana: The Technology of Mental Re-Architecture

If the subconscious mind is the hardware of our existence and the *Samskaras* are the software viruses, then **Sadhana** is the process of re-coding. Many people remain trapped in depression because they try to think their way out of it. However, intellectual thought is a function of the conscious mind—the mere 10% of our awareness that sits above the surface. To truly heal, we must reach the 90% that lies beneath. We must stop being victims of our default mode network and become the active architects of our internal reality.

The Default Mode Network (DMN) is a collection of brain regions that become active when we are not focused on the outside world. In the depressed mind, the DMN is hyper-active, constantly looping through past regrets, future anxieties, and the hypocrisy. We are caught in a self-referential loop where the "Ideal Self" is perpetually judging the "Real Self." **Sadhana** is the intervention that breaks this loop. It is a technological application of spiritual principles designed to bypass the analytical mind and speak directly to the nervous system.

The Power of Spiritual Discipline

In the Vedantic tradition, *Sadhana* is a committed, daily discipline aimed at a specific goal. Depression creates a habit of the mind—a default setting of scanning for threats, failures, and hopelessness. This habit is reinforced every time we flow into the deep canyons of old *Samskaras*. Through *Sadhana*, we introduce a stronger, more vibrant frequency that eventually overrides the old signal. This is not about forced positivity; it is about **neuroplasticity through spirit**.

When we perform a Kriya, chant a Mantra, or hold a Mudra, we are sending a physical and energetic command to the nervous system. We are telling the body: *The old script is no longer valid. I am writing a new one.* Over time, the grooves of peace and presence become deeper than the grooves of despair. The **doorway to awakening** is not something you find; it is something you build, brick by brick, through daily effort.

The Three Pillars of Rewriting

To successfully re-architect the mind, we must utilize the three primary tools of the soul

1. Vibration (Mantra)

Using specific sound frequencies to shatter the static of negative thought loops. Depression often has a sound—a low, repetitive drone of self-criticism. A Mantra replaces this drone with a sacred vibration. As you chant, the physical vibration in the palate and the cranium begins to loosen the sediment of old impressions, making them easier to wash away.

2. Rhythm (Pranayama)

Using the breath to regulate the nervous system and move out of the "Freeze" state (parasympathetic collapse) often associated with depression. In the shadow on tender minds, the breath becomes shallow and erratic. By imposing a conscious rhythm on the breath, we send a signal of safety to the amygdala. We are manually overriding the biological red alert and replacing it with the rhythm of life.

3. Stillness (Dhyana)

Creating a space where the "Witness" can observe the old scripts without being governed by them. In stillness, we realize we are the screen, not the movie. This is the ultimate "graduation" from the educational depression discussed in Chapter 8. We stop being useful to the old script and start being present for the new one.

The Alchemy of Repetition

The software viruses of the mind were not installed in a day; they were the result of years of domestic instability and inherited debt. Therefore, the rewriting process requires a relentless consistency. Each session of

Sadhana is a software update. You may not see the results after one day, but after forty days of consistent practice, the biological mirror of the brain begins to change. The fragile foundation is replaced by a temple of intentional practice.

By committing to this internal work, you decouple from the ancestral shadow. You realize that while you were given a script of gloom, you hold the pen for the next act. This is the transition from loneliness to spiritualism and depression to awakening: the moment the "Silent Witness" takes over the "Director's Chair" of your life.

"We must recognize that mental health is not a separate issue from the way we live; it is woven into the fabric of our expectations, our values, and our relationships."

— *Suman Saran Sinha*

Points for Introspection

To begin your own "Mental Re-Architecture," reflect deeply on these points:

1. **Identifying the "Background Drone":** Close your eyes and listen to your internal dialogue. If your depression had a sound or a vibration, what would it be? Is it a high-pitched whine of anxiety or a low, heavy thud of despair?

2. **The 10% vs. 90% Reality:** Think of a time you tried to talk yourself out of a bad mood. Did it work? Acknowledge the limitation of the 10% conscious mind. How does it feel to realize that the re-coding must happen at a deeper, non-verbal level?

3. **Selecting Your First "Brick":** Look at the Three Pillars (Vibration, Rhythm, Stillness). Which one feels most accessible to you right now? Commit to practicing just five minutes of that pillar every day this week.

4. **The "Software Update" Log:** For the next seven days, note how you feel *immediately after* a period of stillness or deep breathing. Do not judge the day as a whole; just note the microscopic shift in the Default Mode Network.

5. **Recognizing the "Old Script" Trigger:** Identify one specific situation that usually crashes your mental software (e.g., a certain person's comment, a financial worry). When this happens, can you pause and say, *"This is just an old script running*?"

6. **The Vision of the Temple:** If your mind were a temple instead of a survival bunker, what would the atmosphere feel like? Describe the frequency you want to live in—not as a goal for the future, but as a vibration you are beginning to invite in today.

21-Day Kriya: The Shield of Light (Kavacha Kriya)

This Kriya is designed to create a "protective boundary" around the mind, preventing external negativity and old subconscious scripts from taking root.

- **The Physical Seat:** Sit with a tall spine. Cross your arms over your chest, tucking your hands into your armpits (this is a grounding posture that signals safety to the brain's limbic system).
- **The Breath:** *Kumbhaka* (Breath Retention). Inhale deeply, hold the breath for as long as comfortable (without straining), and exhale slowly.
- **The 21-Day Progression**
    - **Days 1–7 (Cleansing):** During the inhale, imagine a brilliant white light entering through the crown of your head. During the hold, feel this light scrubbing the inside of your skull, clearing away the grey fog of old scripts.
    - **Days 8–14 (Building the Shield):** As you exhale, imagine the white light expanding out of your pores to form a radiant Shield (Kavacha) one foot around your body. Mentally repeat: *I am protected. I am whole.*
    - **Days 15–21 (The Mantra Seal):** Add the Bija mantra **"HUM"** (the sound of protection and cutting through illusion). Repeat the sound 21 times while visualizing the shield growing stronger and more impenetrable.
- **The Goal:** To move from a state of vulnerability to a state of sovereignty, where the old depression scripts can no longer find a hook in your consciousness.

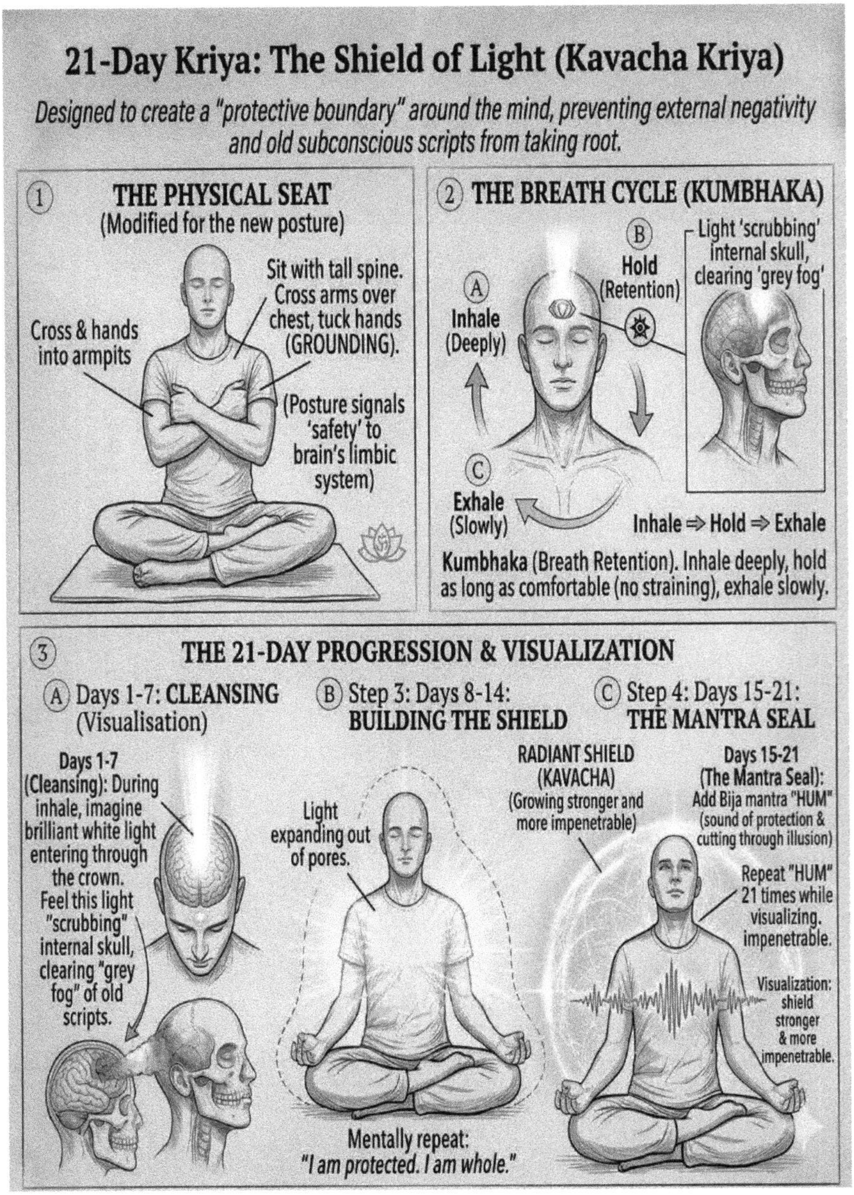
21-Day Kriya: The Shield of Light (Kavacha Kriya)
Designed to create a "protective boundary" around the mind, preventing external negativity and old subconscious scripts from taking root.
1 THE PHYSICAL SEAT
(Modified for the new posture)
Sit with tall spine. Cross arms over chest, tuck hands (GROUNDING).
Cross & hands into armpits
(Posture signals 'safety' to brain's limbic system)
2 THE BREATH CYCLE (KUMBHAKA)
A Inhale (Deeply)
B Hold (Retention)
Light 'scrubbing' internal skull, clearing 'grey fog'
C Exhale (Slowly)
Inhale ⇒ Hold ⇒ Exhale
Kumbhaka (Breath Retention). Inhale deeply, hold as long as comfortable (no straining), exhale slowly.
3 THE 21-DAY PROGRESSION & VISUALIZATION
A Days 1-7: CLEANSING (Visualisation)
B Step 3: Days 8-14: BUILDING THE SHIELD
C Step 4: Days 15-21: THE MANTRA SEAL
Days 1-7 (Cleansing): During inhale, imagine brilliant white light entering through the crown. Feel this light "scrubbing" internal skull, clearing "grey fog" of old scripts.
Light expanding out of pores.
Mentally repeat: "I am protected. I am whole."
RADIANT SHIELD (KAVACHA) (Growing stronger and more impenetrable)
Days 15-21 (The Mantra Seal): Add Bija mantra "HUM" (sound of protection & cutting through illusion)
Repeat "HUM" 21 times while visualizing. impenetrable.
Visualization: shield stronger & more impenetrable.

Chapter - 10
The Infinite Presence

The Arrival: Living from the Soul

The journey through the philosophy of depression is not a race to a finish line where the old you are waiting. Instead, it is a process of shedding every layer of identity that was never yours to begin with. We have walked through the domestic shadows, the societal pressures of independence, the financial anxieties, and the subconscious software viruses. Now, we stand at the threshold. The doorway is no longer something you are looking *at*; it is something you have become. This is the state of **Spiritualism**—the realization that you are not a human being having a spiritual crisis, but a spiritual being navigating a human experience.

Arrival in this context is not a geographic destination, but a shift in the seat of your consciousness. When you live from the soul, the "Inherited Debts" of Chapter 1 no longer dictate your worth. You recognize that the "Fragile Foundation" of your childhood was merely the terrain, not the architect. The arrival is the moment of radical self-governance, where you finally close the book on generations of gloom and begin to write a script based on your infinite nature.

The Still Point of the Turning World

In the depths of loneliness, the ego feels like a drowning man. In the heights of Spiritualism, the soul feels like the ocean itself. This chapter explores the concept of ***Jivanmukti***—liberation while still in the body. To be liberated does not mean you will never feel sadness again; it means you are no longer *defined* by that sadness. You have found the Still Point. Just as the hub of a wheel remains stationary while the spokes spin in a blur of activity, your inner Witness remains unshaken by the ups and downs of worldly life.

The Still Point is the discovery of the "Silent Witness" introduced in Chapter 5. It is the realization that while the pall of gloom may occasionally pass over the sun of your being, it cannot extinguish it. This is the ultimate "Dis-identification." You observe the depression not as a catastrophe, but as a weather pattern. You hold your sadness with the same tenderness a mother holds a crying child—knowing that the child is crying but also knowing that the child is fundamentally safe.

Transmuting the Void into Fullness

When you live from the **Infinite Presence**, your loneliness turned depression is transmuted into All-Oneness. The void that once felt like a terrifying emptiness is now recognized as a "Fullness"—a space teeming with potential, peace, and connection to the Divine. You no longer seek a cure for your depression because you have realized that the depression was the very fire that burned away the dross, leaving only the pure gold of your eternal nature.

This transmutation is the alchemy of the soul. The "Myth of Independence" from Chapter 2 is replaced by the reality of Universal Interdependence. You see that the social reasons for your despair were invitations to reclaim the philosophy of Dharma. In the state of Fullness, you are never alone because you are connected to the Source of all things. The Prison of Isolation dissolves because the walls were made of an ego that no longer governs your reality.

The Return to the World

Awakening is not an exit strategy; it is a way of re-entry. You return to your family, your work, and your social circles, but you move with a different frequency. You are no longer driven by the hypocrisy or the need for external validation. You act from a place of **Service and Presence**. You become a Doorway for others, showing them through your very existence that the dark night of the soul is not a destination, but a rite of passage.

Your return is marked by the "Re-Architecture" of Chapter 9. Your daily life becomes a continuous **Sadhana**, where every action is a software update of peace. You move through the "Cubicle" world with the heart of the "Village," practicing your **Dharma** regardless of the external environment. You are in the world, but no longer *of* the gloom. You have graduated from the education of the soul and now serve as a living curriculum for those still wandering in the dark.

"True independence is a myth; interdependence is the reality of the universe. When we look at the cosmos, nothing exists in isolation."

— *Suman Saran Sinha*

Points for Introspection

To anchor yourself in the **Infinite Presence** and finalize your Awakening, reflect on these final points:

1. **The State of the Gateway:** Look back at Chapter 1. Do you still feel like a victim of the family script, or can you feel the Light of Awareness beginning to decouple you from those inherited patterns?

2. **Locating the Still Point:** During your next moment of stress or sadness, can you find the hub of the wheel? Can you feel the part of you that remains stationary and unshaken while your emotions spin around it?

3. **Transmutation Audit:** Identify one dark aspect of your depression (e.g., the loneliness, the emptiness). How can you reframe that today as a Fullness or a Sacred Clearing that allowed your spiritual nature to finally emerge?

4. **The Frequency of Re-entry:** As you prepare to return to the world, what is the specific different frequency you want to project? How will your interactions with your family or colleagues change now that you are no longer seeking their validation?

5. **Becoming the Doorway:** Who in your life is currently wandering in the dark? Without using words, how can your mere *presence*—your stillness and your peace—serve as a doorway for them?

6. **The Gold vs. The Dross:** List three ways that your Dark Night of the Soul has strengthened your character. What pure gold has remained after the fire of depression burned away the dross of your old identity?

21-Day Kriya: The Infinite Stillness (Samadhi Kriya)

This final Kriya is designed to integrate all previous lessons into a single state of Unshakable Peace.

- **The Physical Seat:** Sit in your most stable meditative posture (*Padmasana* or *Sukhasana*). Imagine your spine as a pillar of light connecting the Earth to the Heavens.
- **The Mudra:** *Bhairava Mudra* (Right hand resting on top of the left, both palms facing up). This represents the union of the individual and the universal.
- **The 21-Day Progression**
  - **Days 1–7 (The Quietness):** Sit in absolute silence for 20 minutes. Do not use a technique. If a thought arises, simply note "Thinking" and return to the silence.
  - **Days 8–14 (The Light):** Visualize a tiny spark of light at the heart center. With every inhale, see it expand to fill your body. With every exhale, see it expand to fill the room, the city, and the universe.
  - **Days 15–21 (The Integration):** Practice "Open-Eyed Meditation." Sit for 10 minutes looking at the world around you, while maintaining the internal "Still Point." Recognize that the world outside and the spirit inside are one.
- **The Goal:** To anchor the realization that you are the **Infinite Presence**, regardless of the changing weather of your mind.

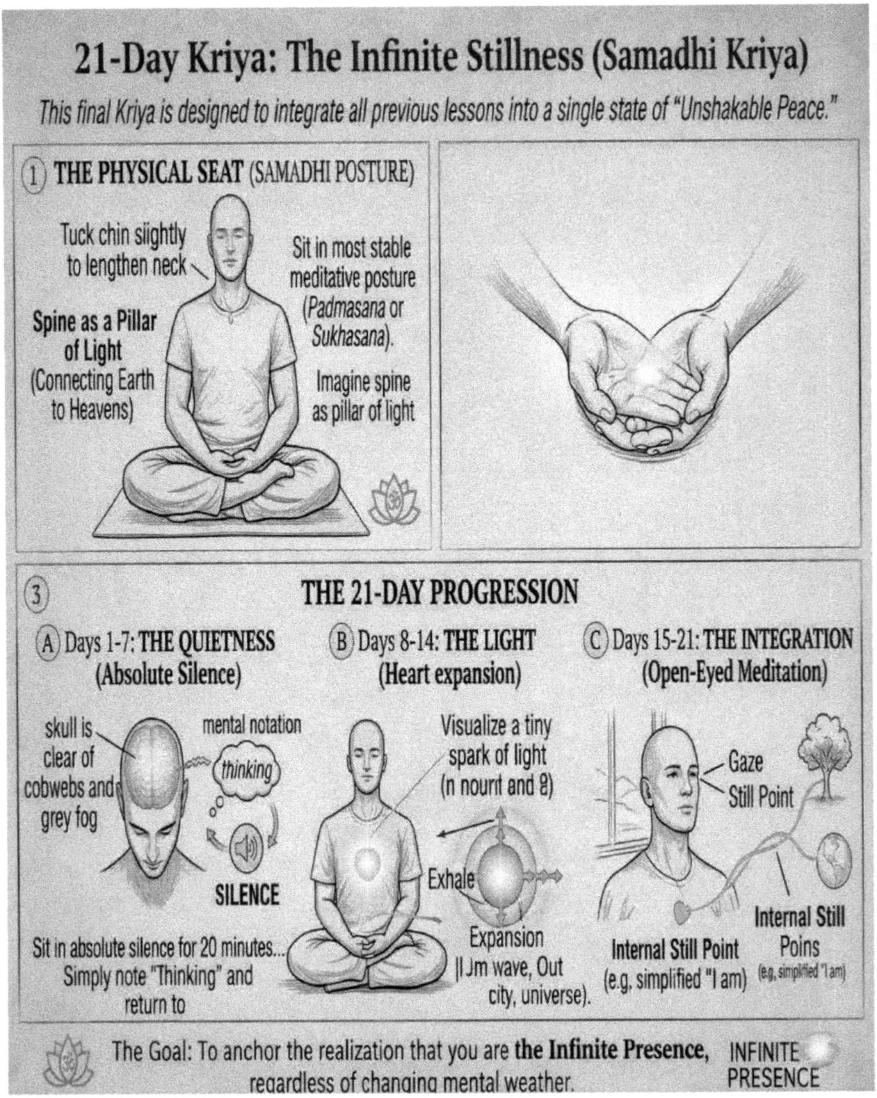
21-Day Kriya: The Infinite Stillness (Samadhi Kriya)
This final Kriya is designed to integrate all previous lessons into a single state of "Unshakable Peace."
1 THE PHYSICAL SEAT (SAMADHI POSTURE)
Tuck chin siightly to lengthen neck
Sit in most stable meditative posture (Padmasana or Sukhasana).
Spine as a Pillar of Light (Connecting Earth to Heavens)
Imagine spine as pillar of light
3 THE 21-DAY PROGRESSION
A Days 1-7: THE QUIETNESS (Absolute Silence)
B Days 8-14: THE LIGHT (Heart expansion)
C Days 15-21: THE INTEGRATION (Open-Eyed Meditation)
skull is clear of cobwebs and grey fog
mental notation
thinking
SILENCE
Sit in absolute silence for 20 minutes... Simply note "Thinking" and return to
Visualize a tiny spark of light (n nourıt and 8)
Exhale
Expansion (|Jm wave, Out city, universe).
Gaze
Still Point
Internal Still Point (e.g, simplified "I am)
Internal Still Poins (e.g, simplified "I am)
The Goal: To anchor the realization that you are the Infinite Presence, regardless of changing mental weather.
INFINITE PRESENCE

Epilogue
The Dawn of the Unconditioned Self

The Final Transmutation: From Why to Is

We began this journey in the suffocating pall of gloom, dissecting the inherited debts of our childhood and the fragile foundations of a life built on sand. We traveled through the cubicles of artificial isolation and the exhausting theater of the Ideal Self. We examined the software viruses of the subconscious and the heavy weight of an education that taught us how to labor but not how to be. Now, as the final pages of this inquiry turn, we move beyond the "Why" of our suffering and step firmly into the "Is" of our eternal nature.

The philosophy of depression was never meant to be a permanent residence; it was a map used to navigate the dark forest of the ego. But a map is not the territory. The territory is the **Infinite Presence**—the vast, unconditioned awareness that remains when every story you have ever told yourself about your brokenness finally falls away.

The Gift of the Great Dissolution

In the beginning, your loneliness felt like a prison. You viewed your depression as a malfunction, a shameful secret, or a biological betrayal. But as we have explored, this Great Dissolution was a form of grace. It was the Silent Witness within you systematically dismantling the hypocrisy. The depression was the fire, yes—but it only burned what was combustible. It burned the masks, the attachments, and the false identities you inherited from a domestic atmosphere of instability.

What remains after the fire is the pure gold of your eternal nature. You have discovered that the "Void" you so feared was not an empty grave, but a **Sacred Clearing**. In that clearing, for the first time in your life, you are free to build a foundation of stone. You are no longer paying interest on the emotional debts of your ancestors because you have performed the radical act of **Ancestral Decoupling**. You have graduated from the Industrial Model of the Mind and entered the Education of the Soul.

The Practice of All-Oneness

As you move forward, the transition from depression to spiritualism manifests as a shift from "Me" to "We." The "Myth of Independence" that once drove you into a "Prison of Isolation" has been replaced by the Vedantic truth of **Dharma**—the realization that your well-being is inextricably linked to the Universal Whole. You no longer seek to be self-made; you seek to be God-realized or Source-aligned.

This All-Oneness is the antidote to the phantom pain of the severed limb. When you act from the **Still Point**, you are no longer a drowning man in a sea of loneliness; you are the ocean itself witnessing its own waves. Your life becomes a **Sadhana**—not a chore to be completed, but a technology of mental re-architecture that keeps your frequency high and your software clean.

The Living Doorway: Your Re-entry

Awakening is not a departure from the world, but a more profound engagement with it. You will still walk through the "Cubicles," you will still navigate Financial Existential Crises, and you may even feel the pall of gloom drift across your horizon from time to time. But you will do so with a **Different Frequency**.

You are no longer a victim of the Subconscious Script. You are the "Silent Witness" who sees the Software Virus and chooses not to run the code. You have found the "Still Point of the Turning World." By simply existing in this state of **Presence and Service**, you become a Doorway for others. Your presence tells them: *I have been where you are. I have felt that weight. And I am here to tell you that there is light on the other side.*

Living After the Storm

There is a common misconception that healing is the return to a previous state. We imagine that recovery means becoming the person we once were before the darkness arrived. Yet the deeper truth is that no significant inner journey ends with a return. It ends with a transformation.

The storm changes the landscape.

When depression first enters our lives, we often experience it as an enemy. It disrupts our ambitions, weakens our confidence, strains relationships, and steals the colours from the world. We naturally long for its departure. We want our old life back. We want certainty restored. We want to feel as we once did.

But as the journey unfolds, something unexpected begins to occur. The very questions that caused discomfort become sources of insight. The silence that once felt oppressive becomes a place of reflection. The loneliness that once felt like abandonment becomes an opportunity for self-discovery.

The storm leaves scars, but it also leaves wisdom.

Many seekers discover that after emerging from a period of profound suffering, they can no longer live as they once did. The old pursuits lose some of their fascination. The endless race for recognition appears less urgent. The need to impress others gradually weakens. One begins to value authenticity over appearance, depth over distraction, and meaning over achievement.

This does not mean life becomes perfect.

Challenges continue to arise. Moments of sadness still visit. Uncertainty remains a companion of human existence. The difference is that we no longer interpret every difficulty as a catastrophe. We understand that darkness and light belong to the same rhythm of life.

The awakened individual does not become immune to suffering. Rather, he develops a different relationship with it.

He ceases to ask, "Why is this happening to me?" and begins to ask,

"What is this experience asking me to understand?"

This subtle shift changes everything.

The storm teaches humility. It reveals the limits of control. It exposes the fragility of the identities we construct around success, status, and approval. Most importantly, it introduces us to a deeper dimension of ourselves that remains untouched by circumstances.

Within every human being there exists a silent center—a witnessing presence that observes both joy and sorrow. During ordinary times we rarely notice it. The noise of life keeps our attention occupied elsewhere. Yet suffering has a strange gift: it strips away distractions and forces us inward.

What we discover there is not despair.

We discover awareness.

And awareness changes the nature of our existence.

The goal of this journey was never merely to eliminate pain. Pain, after all, is an inevitable part of life. The true goal is to awaken to a level of consciousness that is larger than pain, larger than fear, and larger than the temporary dramas of the mind.

Living after the storm means carrying this awareness into everyday life.

It means drinking a cup of tea with gratitude.

It means listening more deeply.

It means forgiving more easily.

It means recognizing that every person we meet is carrying unseen burdens and fighting silent battles.

Most of all, it means understanding that healing is not a destination reached once and forever. It is a continuous relationship with truth, presence, and self-understanding.

The storm may have passed, but its greatest gift remains.

It showed us that beneath every fear, every wound, and every uncertainty, there exists a light that was never damaged by the darkness.

To live after the storm is to remember that light.

And to allow it to illuminate the path ahead.

Final Blessing: The Light That Never Fails

May you never again mistake the fog for the sky. May you remember that your Fragile Foundation has been replaced by the Infinite Presence. You are not a depressed person trying to find God; you are the **Divine Self** observing a human journey of transformation.

The doorway is open. Step through. The awakening you sought has been waiting for you all along; hidden in the very silence you once feared. You are Home.

"You can read a thousand books on peace, but until you experience the silence between two thoughts, you remain uneducated in peace."

— *Suman Saran Sinha*

Final Points for Introspection

To seal the wisdom of this journey as you conclude the book, reflect on these final inquiries:

1. **The Identity Shift:** If you were to introduce yourself today, not by your name, your job, or your history, but by your Essential Nature, what words would you use? Notice how it feels to let go of the Industrial Identity.

2. **The Gratitude of the Void:** Look back at your darkest moment of loneliness. Can you now find one reason to be grateful for that emptiness? How did that "Void" specifically prepare the space for your current "Fullness?"

3. **The Commitment to Sadhana:** What is the one Internal Software Update (Mantra, Breath, or Stillness) you commit to performing every single day to ensure the old script never takes root again?

4. **The Legacy of Peace:** Now that you have decoupled from Generations of Gloom, what is the New Inheritance you wish to leave for those who come after you? What Samskaras of peace are you writing today?

5. **The Witness in Action:** Tomorrow, when you face a Weight of Uncertainty or a social pressure, can you pause and find the Still Point for just ten seconds? How does that small pause change your reaction?

6. **The Final Surrender:** What is the very last mask or Ideal Self-image you are still clinging to? Are you ready to let it go into the fire and trust the pure gold that remains?

SALVATION

The mind is a cage of gilded bars,
Where we count our wounds and hide our scars.

But look through the crack where the light creeps in,
To the place where the soul and the stars begin.

The door was never locked, my friend,
The journey is where the struggles end.

Step through the shadow, leave the fear,
The home you sought was always here.

"You are not the shadow that passed through your mind.
You are the sky through which it travelled."

— Suman Saran Sinha

"Depression is not always the absence of strength. Sometimes it is the exhaustion of carrying invisible burdens for too long."

— Suman Saran Sinha

Conversations with the Silence

On Loneliness

Loneliness becomes unbearable when we interpret it as abandonment. It becomes transformative when we encounter it as an invitation to meet ourselves. The room has not become empty; it has become quite enough for us to hear what was always speaking beneath the noise.

On Waiting

Much of human suffering arises from the belief that life should unfold according to our timetable. Yet the deepest transformations rarely arrive when demanded. The seed does not bloom because it is impatient. It blooms because the season is right.

On Failure

Failure wounds the ego because it challenges the image, we have created of ourselves. Yet life is rarely interested in protecting our image. It is interested in revealing our essence. What falls away was never truly ours.

On Exhaustion

Sometimes exhaustion is not the result of doing too much. It is the result of carrying too many masks. The soul grows weary when it must constantly pretend to be someone it is not.

On Silence

Silence is often misunderstood as the absence of something. In reality, it is the presence of everything that becomes visible when distractions disappear. It is not empty. It is full beyond measure.

On Fear

Fear is the imagination rehearsing a future that has not yet arrived. Most of the suffering it creates exists only in possibility. Awareness returns us to the only place where life is actually happening: this moment.

On Comparison

The flower does not compare itself with the tree. The river does not envy the mountain. Only the human mind measures its worth by looking sideways. Peace begins when we return our attention to our own unfolding.

On Meaning

Meaning is not discovered in extraordinary moments alone. It is often hidden within ordinary acts performed with sincerity, attention, and love. A meaningful life is rarely dramatic. It is deeply authentic.

On Uncertainty

We seek certainty because we believe it will bring security. Yet uncertainty is not a flaw in existence; it is one of its fundamental conditions. To embrace uncertainty is to participate fully in life rather than merely negotiate with it.

On Hope

Hope is not the conviction that tomorrow will be easy. It is the quiet trust that even difficult experiences can contribute to our growth. It is courage disguised as patience.

On Forgiveness

Forgiveness does not erase memory. It releases us from becoming prisoners of memory. The past may remain unchanged, but our relationship to it can be transformed.

On Achievement

Achievement satisfies a goal. Fulfilment nourishes a life. The two are not always the same. One can accumulate achievements and remain empty or live simply and feel profoundly complete.

On Belonging

The deepest longing of the human heart is not for success, admiration, or power. It is for belonging. Not merely belonging to a family, a nation, or a community, but belonging to existence itself.

On Suffering

Suffering often appears meaningless while we are passing through it. Only later do we recognize how it expanded our compassion, deepened our understanding, and revealed strengths we never knew we possessed.

On Awakening

Awakening is not the acquisition of something new. It is the gradual recognition of what has always been present. The journey ends where it began, but we return with different eyes.

On the Light

The light we seek is rarely found at the end of the road. It accompanies us throughout the journey, hidden beneath fear, obscured by doubt, and forgotten in moments of despair. Awakening is simply the remembrance of what was never lost.

"To understand the Silent Witness, we must distinguish between the Content of consciousness and the Container of consciousness."

— Suman Saran Sinha

Appendix - 1

The 21-Day Kriya Roadmap

Phase	Kriya Name	Core Purpose	Key Visual Element
1. Grounding	**Prithvi Sthiti** (Earth Seat)	Grounding the nervous system; replacing "shaky" foundations.	Roots extending from sit-bones into the bedrock.
2. Connection	**Hridaya Kriya** (Heart Connection)	Breaking the ego shell; expanding heart awareness.	Golden thread connecting your heart to others/the whole.
3. Abundance	**Artha Shuddhi** (Abundance Flow)	Shifting from Scarcity Mode to Purpose Mode.	Golden sun rising in the solar plexus; burning grey fog.
4. Internal Truth	**Satya Kriya** (Mirror of Truth)	Withdrawing from external validation; seeing the "Witness."	Mirror meditation; Hakini Mudra integrating the "split" self.

5. Subconscious	**Bhramari** (Subconscious Reset)	Planting new seeds; bypassing the critical ego-mind.	Bee breath vibrations "shaking loose" skull tension.
6. Ancestral	**Pitru Shuddhi** (Ancestral Release)	Releasing inherited weight; balancing masculine/feminine.	Circle of white light; bowing to ancestors from a place of sovereignty.
7. Intuition	**Gyana Kriya** (Wisdom Eye)	Activating the Third Eye; moving toward direct wisdom.	Clearing "cobwebs" of useless data; focusing on the Ajna Chakra.
8. Sovereignty	**Kavacha Kriya** (Shield of Light)	Creating a protective boundary against negativity.	Radiant shield one foot around the body; white light "scrubbing."
9. Integration	**Samadhi Kriya** (Infinite Stillness)	Anchoring the realization of Infinite Presence.	Spine as a pillar of light; the union of inner and outer worlds.

Appendix - 2

Introduction to Sadhana

The Technology of Awakening

The journey from depression to awakening is not a passive one; it is a transition from being a victim of your circumstances to becoming the scientist of your own consciousness. While the preceding chapters have provided the philosophical map of the pall of gloom, this appendix serves as the laboratory manual. To move through the doorway to awakening, one must engage in ***Sadhana***—a committed spiritual practice designed to re-architect the mind and purge the software viruses of depression.

I. The Science of Sadhana: Why Discipline Works

In the modern era, we are often taught that healing should be easy, instantaneous, or purely medicinal. However, the samskara teaches us that our depression is held in deep, structural grooves in the subconscious mind. These grooves were carved by years of domestic instability and inherited debt. You cannot think your way out of a canyon; you must build a path out of it.

Sadhana is the intentional creation of new, positive "*Para-Samskaras.*" By repeating specific actions, breaths, and sounds, you are performing a manual override of your nervous system. This is neuroplasticity in its most sacred form. You are not just praying for relief; you are using the technology of the soul to change the frequency of your biological mirror.

II. The Three Pillars of Your Practice

To successfully rewrite your subconscious script, your *Sadhana* must address the three layers of your being: the Body, the Breath, and the Mind.

1. The Pillar of Vibration (Mantra)

Depression has a sound—a low, repetitive drone of self-criticism and performative exhaustion. **Mantra** is the use of sacred sound to shatter this static.

- **The Mechanism:** When you chant, the vibration hits the 84 meridian points on the roof of the mouth, sending signals to the hypothalamus and changing the chemistry of the brain.
- **The Practice:** Choose a mantra that resonates with your Still Point, such as *Sat Nam* (Truth is my Identity) or *So Hum* (I am That).
- **The Goal:** To replace the inherited script with a universal frequency that the ego cannot corrupt.

The Pillar of Rhythm (Pranayama)

The Shadow on Tender Minds often manifests as a frozen nervous system—a state of biological red alert that never stands down. **Pranayama** (breath control) is the tool used to thaw this freeze.

- **The Mechanism:** By consciously slowing the breath, you stimulate the Vagus nerve, moving the body from Survival Mode to Peace Mode.
- **The Practice:** Long Deep Breathing or Alternate Nostril Breathing serves as a software update for your internal regulator.
- **The Goal:** To prove to your subconscious that you are safe in the present moment, regardless of the weight of uncertainty in the external world.

2. The Pillar of Stillness (Dhyana)

Stillness is where you meet the **Silent Witness**. In depression, we are terrified of silence because we fear the void. **Dhyana** (meditation) teaches us that the void is a Fullness.

- **The Mechanism:** By sitting in stillness, you stop feeding the "DMN" (Default Mode Network) and start identifying with the "Observer."

- **The Practice:** Sitting silently and watching thoughts float by like leaves on a river, without reaching out to grab them.
- **The Goal:** To realize that you are the screen, not the tragedy projected upon it.

III. Designing Your 40-Day Transformation

In spiritual technology, it takes 40 days to break a habit and 90 days to establish a new one. To move from depression to awareness, you must commit to a 40-day *Sadhana*. This is the rite of passage that turns the hypocrisy into the philosophy of truth.

The Daily Curriculum

1. **Preparation (5 Minutes):** Create a "Temple" in your home—a small, well ventilated, clean space dedicated to your awakening.
2. **Tuning In (2 Minutes):** Acknowledge the "Inherited Debts" you are setting down for this time.
3. **Breathwork (11 Minutes):** Use rhythmic breathing to clear the "pall of gloom" from your nervous system.
4. **Mantra (11 Minutes):** Vibrate the sound that rewrites your "subconscious script."
5. **Stillness (5 Minutes):** Rest in the "Infinite Presence" of the Silent Witness.

IV. The Alchemy of Consistency

The greatest obstacle to *Sadhana* is the ego's desire for Industrial Efficiency. Your mind will tell you that you are too tired, that it isn't working, or that you have more important things to do. This is the Software Virus trying to protect itself.

Remember: **Sadhana is not a chore; it is a love letter to your Soul.** Every minute you spend in practice is a brick in your foundation of stone. You are not doing this to become better; you are doing this to shed the dross and reveal the pure gold that has always been there.

Points for Introspection: Your Sadhana Blueprint

1. **Selecting Your Tools:** Based on the Three Pillars, which specific practice (Mantra, Breath, or Stillness) feels like the most powerful anti-virus for your current state of mind?
2. **Identifying the Saboteur:** What is the specific script your ego uses to avoid discipline? (e.g., *"I'll start tomorrow," "This is silly"*) Recognize this as a mechanical survival response, not a truth.
3. **The Space of the Temple:** Look around your living environment. Where can you establish a physical doorway to awakening—a corner where the pall of gloom is not allowed to enter?
4. **Defining the Goal:** Beyond feeling better, what is the Infinite Presence you wish to invite into your life? How will your re-entry into the world look once you have completed your 40 days?
5. **The Witness of Resistance:** When you feel the urge to quit your practice, can you step back and observe that resistance? Ask the Witness: *"Who is the one feeling resistant?"* Notice that the Witness is always ready to practice.
6. **The Ancestral Gift:** By committing to this Sadhana, you are not just healing yourself; you are closing the book on generations of gloom. How does it feel to realize your discipline is a gift to your entire lineage?

"The mind suffers most when it becomes disconnected from silence, meaning, and authentic inner life."

— Suman Saran Sinha

Appendix - 3

Practice

11-Minute Meditation for Clearing the Ancestral Shadow

This practice is a specific **Sadhana** designed to bypass the 10% analytical mind and reach the 90% subconscious "basement" where **Inherited Emotional Debts** reside. By using **Vibration (Mantra)** and **Rhythm (Pranayama)**, we create a Sacred Clearing in the nervous system.

Phase 1: Tuning In (1 Minute)

- **The Posture:** Sit with a Foundation of Stone—spine straight, chest slightly lifted, and chin tucked in to create a doorway for energy to flow.
- **The Intent:** Mentally acknowledge the pall of gloom you have carried for your lineage. State internally: *"I am the Silent Witness. I am here to close the book on generations of gloom."*

Phase 2: The Breath of Decoupling (4 Minutes)

In this phase, we address the **Fragile Foundation** of the nervous system.

- **The Technique:** Inhale deeply through the nose in 4 powerful sniffs. As you inhale, imagine pulling the grey energy of inherited sorrow out of your cells.
- **The Exhale:** Exhale in one long, forceful breath through puckered lips (as if blowing through a straw), projecting the weight of uncertainty out of your field.
- **The Philosophy:** You are manually overriding the biological red alert of your ancestors and replacing it with your own sovereign rhythm.

Phase 3: The Mantra of Re-Architecture (5 Minutes)

Now, we use **Vibration** to rewrite the "Subconscious Script."

- **The Mantra:** We use the sounds **SA-TA-NA-MA**.
  - **SA:** Birth/Infinity (The Infinite Presence)
  - **TA:** Life/Existence (Dharma)
  - **NA:** Death/Transformation (The Great Dissolution)
  - **MA:** Rebirth/Awakening (The Doorway)
- **The Movement:** With each syllable, press a different finger to your thumb:
  - **SA:** Index finger (Knowledge/Vidya)
  - **TA:** Middle finger (Patience/Dharma)
  - **NA:** Ring finger (Vitality/Prana)
  - **MA:** Pinky finger (Communication/Presence)
- **The Visualization:** Imagine a beam of light entering the top of your head (the L-shape flow), washing away the Software Viruses and leaving only the pure gold of your eternal nature.

Phase 4: The Still Point (1 Minute)

- **The Silence:** Stop the movement and the mantra. Sit in absolute stillness.
- **The Observation:** Become the **Silent Witness**. Observe the space where the shadow used to be. Notice that the "Void" has become a "Fullness."
- **The Closing:** Take a deep breath, stretch your arms up to claim your space in the world, and exhale powerfully.

Points for Introspection: After the Practice

1. **The Physical Shift:** Immediately after the 11 minutes, does your body feel heavier or lighter? Does the pall of gloom feel like a structural part of you, or just a passing cloud?
2. **The Sound of the Script:** During the mantra, did the background drone of self-criticism get louder or quieter? Did you feel the vibration loosening the sediment of old impressions?
3. **The Witness Perspective:** In the final minute of stillness, were you able to see the depression as a movie on a screen rather than a tragedy you were drowning in?
4. **The Ancestral Reaction:** Did a specific face or memory from your childhood arise during the Breath of Decoupling? How does it feel to return the debt to that image with a sense of peace?
5. **The Strength of the Foundation:** Do you feel more like a victim of the family script or the Architect of the Temple after this session?
6. **The Frequency of Re-entry:** How can you carry the Still Point you found in this 11-minute practice into your next interaction with the "Cubicle" world?

"A temple is a space of Samskara (right impressions). It is a place where every action is intentional, every word is mindful, and the atmosphere is curated for peace rather than survival."

— Suman Saran Sinha

Appendix - 4

Glossary of Terms

From the Abyss to the Awakening

A

- **Ancestral Decoupling:** The radical philosophical and energetic act of recognizing that certain sorrows are Inherited Emotional Debts rather than personal failures. It is the process of closing the book on generations of gloom.
- **Artha:** The pursuit of material prosperity and security. In this text, *Artha* is viewed as a foundational necessity that must be aligned with *Dharma* to prevent a Financial Existential Crisis.
- **Atman:** The true, unchanging, and eternal Self. Unlike the Ideal Self or the Ego, the *Atman* is the Silent Witness that remains untouched by the fluctuations of depression.

C

- **Chitta Vritti Nirodha:** The ancient Vedantic goal of stilling the mental whirlpools or fluctuations of the mind. It is the technical objective of rewriting the Subconscious Script.
- **Cubicle Mindset:** A state of Artificial Isolation where life is compartmentalized and the individual is severed from the communal Village.

D

- **Default Mode Network (DMN):** A collection of brain regions active during self-referential thought. In the depressed mind, the DMN becomes a loop of Performative Exhaustion and past regrets.
- **Dharma:** Mutual duty and righteous purpose. It is the glue of the universe that transforms the Prison of Isolation into a sense of belonging and universal interdependence.
- **Domestic Instability:** An environment lacking in *Samskara* (right impressions), leading to a Fragile Foundation and a state of chronic biological red alert in a Tender Mind.

F

- **Fragile Foundation:** A psychological state resulting from a childhood home defined by inconsistency or emotional unavailability, making the adult nervous system prone to collapse under stress.

I

- **Ideal Self:** A curated, digitally filtered avatar created to seek validation. The struggle to maintain this persona leads to performative exhaustion and the philosophy of hypocrisy.
- **Inherited Emotional Debt:** The unrendered grey or sorrow passed down through generations. It is a weight the Tender Mind carries without having signed for it.

J

- **Jivanmukti:** Liberation while still residing in the physical body. It is the Still Point where one is no longer *defined* by the presence of sadness.

L

- **Learned Helplessness:** A state where the correlation between effort and outcome is severed, leading the mind to retreat into a fog of depression as a defense mechanism.

M

- **Mantra:** A tool of Vibration used to shatter the static of negative thought loops and rewrite the subconscious software.

P

- **Pall of Gloom:** The heavy, atmospheric pressure of depression that often begins in the quiet tributaries of childhood.
- **Para-Samskara:** A powerful, intentionally created positive impression formed through *Sadhana* to fill the canyons of old despair.
- **Pranayama:** The Technology of Rhythm involving conscious breathing to regulate the nervous system and move from Survival Mode to Peace Mode.

S

- **Sadhana:** Committed spiritual discipline or Mental Re-Architecture. It is the active process of turning the philosophy of depression into a doorway to awakening.
- **Samskara:** Subconscious grooves or software viruses created by past experiences and domestic atmospheres.
- **Sankalpa:** The power of Will or Intent. Depression is often viewed as the death of *Sankalpa*.
- **Silent Witness (Sakshi):** The Observer part of consciousness that perceives the pall of gloom without being absorbed by it.

V

- **Vidya:** Wisdom and self-knowledge, as opposed to mere industrial data or schooling.

"We are taught the history of the world, but not the history of our own patterns. We are taught the laws of physics, but not the laws of our own emotions."

— Suman Saran Sinha

Appendix - 5

Group Discussion Protocol: "The Circle of Presence"

If you are moving through this book with a group, use these guidelines to maintain a Sacred Clearing:

1. **The Rule of the Witness:** When someone shares their pall of gloom, the group practices **Sakshi Bhav** (witnessing) without offering unsolicited advice or fixing.
2. **Ancestral Honoring:** Begin each session by acknowledging that everyone in the circle is working to decouple from generations of sorrow.
3. **The Silence Break:** Between discussion points, hold 60 seconds of absolute silence to reconnect with the **Still Point**.

"Sadhana is a technological application of spiritual principles designed to bypass the analytical mind and speak directly to the nervous system."

— Suman Saran Sinha

The 40-Day Progress Log (Sample)

Day	The Dominant "Software Virus"	The Sadhana Applied	The Witness Observation
1	*"I am a burden"*	11-Min Ancestral Clearing	*Felt a heavy chest but observed it from the sky.*
20	*"Uncertainty of future"*	Long Deep Breathing	*The weight is still there, but it feels smaller than I am.*
40	*None / Silence*	Stillness (Dhyana)	*The Doorway is open. I am Home.*

"The state of Spiritualism is the realization that you are not a human being having a spiritual crisis, but a spiritual being navigating a human experience."

— Suman Saran Sinha

Appendix - 6

The First Night: A Ritual of Commitment

(Expanded Meditation Script)

This is a 20-minute guided experience to be performed on the evening before the first official day of **Sadhana**. Its purpose is to clear the Fragile Foundation and set a conscious **Sankalpa** (Will/Intent) for the transformation ahead.

Phase I: The Arrival (3 Minutes)

- **The Physical Space:** Sit in your designated Temple area. Light a single candle or incense. This act represents the Silent Witness entering the pall of gloom.
- **The Body:** Sit with a straight spine. Rest your hands on your knees in *Gyan Mudra* (index finger touching thumb). This mudra connects the Individual Self to the Universal Knowledge.
- **The Breath:** Close your eyes. Inhale deeply, feeling the breath hit the back of the throat. Exhale with a sigh, releasing the Industrial Utility of the day.

Phase II: The Ancestral Hand-Off (7 Minutes)

- **The Visualization:** Imagine you are standing in a vast, grey hallway—the Inherited Debt corridor. To your left and right are the figures of your ancestors, stretching back generations.
- **The Observation:** Notice the Software Viruses they are holding—the anxieties, the silences, the fears of survival.

- **The Action:** Mentally address them with the voice of the **Silent Witness**: *"I honor the life you gave me, but I return the sorrow you carried. I am the one who breaks the cycle. I am the Doorway to Awakening."*
- **The Release:** Imagine a heavy, dark cloak falling from your shoulders and dissolving into the floor. Feel the sudden lightness in your chest—the Sacred Clearing.

Phase III: The Implantation of Sankalpa (7 Minutes)

- **The Seed:** Now that the clearing is made, you must plant a new **Para-Samskara**.
- **The Mantra:** Silently repeat your chosen *Sankalpa*. If you do not have one, use: *"I am the Space, not the Shadow. I am the Presence, not the Pain."*
- **The Rhythm:** Inhale the word **SAT** (Truth). Exhale the word **NAM** (Identity).
- **The Internal Landscape:** Imagine this mantra as a golden liquid filling the canyons of your mind. See the jagged edges of your depression being smoothed over by this new frequency.

Phase IV: The 40-Day Vow (3 Minutes)

- **The Promise:** Speak to your Tender Mind as if it were a child. Tell it: "For the next 40 days, I will not abandon you. I will show up at this altar. I will provide the rhythm you lacked."
- **The Seal:** Bring your hands together at the center of your chest in Prayer Pose (Anjali Mudra). Press the thumbs against the sternum—the seat of the soul.
- **The Closing:** Take one final, massive breath. Hold it for 10 seconds, allowing the energy to circulate to every cell. Exhale and bow forward, touching your forehead to the ground if possible, symbolizing the surrender of the Ego to the **Infinite Presence**.

Points for Introspection: After the First Night

1. **The Weight of the Cloak:** When you visualized dropping the ancestral cloak, did you feel a physical sensation of relief? Which part of your body (shoulders, heart, gut) felt the change most deeply?

2. **The Ego's Protest:** Did a voice arise during the "40-Day Vow" saying, *"You won't finish this*?" Recognize that voice as a Software Virus attempting to maintain its grip. How did the **Silent Witness** react to that voice?

3. **The Quality of the Clearing:** In the silence after the meditation, did the Void feel frightening or did it feel like a Fresh Canvas?

4. **The Power of the Name:** Does your Sankalpa (your new mantra) feel like a Utility, or does it feel like Wisdom?

5. **The Body's Memory:** How does your Fragile Foundation feel now that you have consciously claimed your Foundation of Stone?

"When every borrowed identity falls away,
what remains is not emptiness—
but the silent presence that was never broken."

— Suman Saran Sinha

Appendix - 7

The Sanskrit-English Lexicon of Awakening

A—The Foundation

- **Abhyasa (Constant Practice):** The root of *Sadhana*. It is the effort to remain transitionally grounded in the "Still Point" despite the "software viruses" of the mind.
- **Adhikara (Qualification/Eligibility):** The realization that your suffering has qualified you for this awakening. Your depression is not a deficit; it is the prerequisite for depth.
- **Ananda (Bliss):** Not happiness (which is dependent on external *Artha*), but a causeless, internal radiance that remains even when the Ideal Self is exhausted.
- **Anjali Mudra (Prayer Pose):** The physical act of bringing the left (lunar/emotional) and right (solar/rational) sides of the body together at the heart to seal the Fragile Foundation.

B—The State of Being

- **Buddhi (Intellect/Discernment):** The faculty of the mind that allows the **Silent Witness** to distinguish between a Real Feeling and a Software Virus.
- **Bhakti (Devotion):** The emotional fuel for your *Sadhana*. It is the transition from Loneliness (isolation) to Communion (love for the Infinite).

C—The Mental Field

- **Chitta (Consciousness/Mind-Stuff):** The Screen upon which the philosophy of depression is projected.
- **Chitta Vritti (Fluctuations of the Mind):** The waves of anxiety and despair. *Nirodha* is the process of stilling these waves to see the pure gold beneath.

D—The Path

- **Dharana (Concentration):** The initial stage of meditation where you focus the mind on a single **Sankalpa** to prevent it from sliding back into inherited canyons.
- **Dhyana (Meditation):** The sustained flow of the **Silent Witness** toward the **Infinite Presence**.
- **Duhkha (Suffering/Unease):** Literally a bad space (as in a poorly fitted axle of a wheel). Depression is viewed as a structural misalignment (*Duhkha*) that *Sadhana* corrects.

G—The Forces of Nature

- **Gunas (Qualities of Existence):**
  - **Tamas:** Heaviness, darkness, and lethargy (The pall of gloom).
  - **Rajas:** Activity, anxiety, and over-stimulation (The Industrial Utility).
  - **Sattva:** Balance, light, and clarity (The Doorway to Awakening).

K—The Action

- **Kriya (Completed Action):** A specific sequence of breath and movement designed to achieve a specific software update in the nervous system.
- **Kleshas (Afflictions):** The five root causes of suffering, including *Avidya* (ignorance of the true Self) and *Abhinivesha* (fear of the Great Dissolution or death of the ego).

M—The Tools

- **Maya (Illusion):** The philosophy of hypocrisy. The belief that the Ideal Self on the digital screen is more real than the **Atman**.
- **Mudra (Seal/Gesture):** Locking the energy in the hands or body to prevent the Prana (life force) from leaking into Software Viruses.

P—The Life Force

- **Prana (Vital Energy):** The Battery of the soul. Depression is a state of *Pranic* depletion.
- **Pratyahara (Withdrawal of Senses):** Turning the gaze inward, away from the Cubicle World, to find the Village within.

S—The Transformation

- **Samskara (Impressions):** The grooves in the mind-stuff (*Chitta*). Negative *Samskaras* are viruses; positive *Samskaras* are upgrades.
- **Satsang (Company of Truth):** Replacing Artificial Isolation with a community of seekers who honor the **Silent Witness**.
- **Shunya (The Void/Zero):** The state of nothingness felt in depression, which philosophy reinterprets as the Fertile Empty Space before creation.

V—The Wisdom

- **Vairagya (Dispassion/Detachment):** The ability to watch a software virus run without identifying with it. It is the core skill of the **Silent Witness**.
- **Viveka (Discrimination):** The Sword of the soul that cuts through the inherited debt to reveal the True Identity.

Points for Introspection

1. **Guna Analysis:** Looking at the three *Gunas*, do you feel your depression is mostly *Tamasic* (heavy/dark) or is it a *Rajasic* burnout (anxious/exhausted)? How does naming the quality change your approach to healing?
2. **The Maya Mirror:** Can you identify one area where *Maya* (illusion) is currently convincing you that your Ideal Self is your only identity? What happens to that illusion when you invoke *Viveka* (discrimination)?
3. **The Duhkha Diagnosis:** If depression is just a bad space or a misaligned axle, does it feel more like a technical adjustment than a permanent brokenness?
4. **Embracing Shunya:** Can you sit for one minute and feel the *Shunya* (the void) not as a hole, but as a vast, open Sacred Clearing waiting for your new *Sankalpa*?

"Healing rarely arrives suddenly. It unfolds quietly through awareness, compassion, and repeated return to presence."

— Suman Saran Sinha

Appendix - 8

The Seeker's Companion: Integrated Study Guide

Use this guide to anchor the philosophical concepts of depression to spiritualism into your daily life. Each section corresponds to the three parts of your journey: The Investigation, The Doorway, and The Awakening.

Section I: Investigating the Shadows (Chapters 1–4)

- **The Guna Audit:** Reflect on the pall of gloom in your childhood. Was it dominated by ***Tamas*** (heaviness, silence, neglect) or ***Rajas*** (chaos, anxiety, conflict)?

Introspection: How does identifying the *Guna* of your upbringing help you decouple from the **Inherited Emotional Debt** today?

- **Maya and the Mirror:** Look at your digital life. Where does the philosophy of hypocrisy thrive? List three ways your **Ideal Self** (the ego-mask) creates ***Duhkha*** (structural misalignment) in your heart.

- **Dharma vs. Isolation:** We often seek independence but find only a Prison of Isolation.

Introspection: What is one act of ***Dharma*** (mutual duty) you can perform this week that requires you to step out of your Cubicle and back into the Village?

Section II: The Doorway of Transition (Chapters 5–8)

- **The Sakshi Bhav Practice:** Practice being the **Silent Witness** for ten minutes today.

Introspection: When a depressive thought arises, use ***Viveka*** (discrimination). Can you say, *"I see this Chitta Vritti (mental wave), but I am the Atman (the ocean)*?" Does the wave feel smaller when you don't fight it?

- **Samskara Rewriting:** Identify a deep canyon in your subconscious. This is a corrupted ***Samskara***.

Introspection: If you were to plant a ***Para-Samskara*** (a new, powerful impression) to fill that canyon, what would its frequency be? (e.g., Peace, Strength, or Truth).

- **Shunya (The Void):** When the Education of the Soul begins, we often feel empty.

Introspection: Can you reframe this loneliness as ***Shunya***—a sacred, fertile zero-point? What new life is waiting to be born in that clearing?

Section III: Living the Awakening (Chapters 9–10 & Appendixes)

- **The Technology of Sadhana:** You are now an architect. Review the **Three Pillars** in the Appendix.

Introspection: Which tool—***Mantra*** (Vibration), **Pranayama** (Rhythm), or **Dhyana** (Stillness)—feels like the most effective anti-virus for your specific Software Virus today?

- **The Sankalpa Vow:** Your 40-day journey is an act of ***Abhyasa*** (constant practice).

Introspection: When ***Tamas*** (lethargy) tells you to skip your practice, how will your ***Sankalpa*** (willpower) respond? Write down your non-negotiable vow to your ***Atman*** (Soul).

- **Jivanmukti (Liberation):** As you prepare for re-entry into the world, you are practicing being a Living Doorway.

Introspection: How does it feel to know that your ***Duhkha*** was the very thing that qualified you (***Adhikara***) for this depth of ***Ananda*** (bliss)?

Weekly Progress & Vocabulary Tracker

Week	Sanskrit Focus	Philosophical Goal	Lived Experience
1	**Viveka**	Discriminate between the "Shadow" and the "Witness."	*Recognized a parent's voice as a virus.*
2	**Prana**	Build energy through **Pranayama** to lift the "pall."	*Felt less leaden in the mornings.*
3	**Samskara**	Repeat my **Sankalpa** to fill the old canyons.	*The 'broken' script is fading away.*
4	**Ananda**	Experience bliss that doesn't depend on the world.	*Found a Still Point in a busy cubicle.*

"We are educating the intellect while starving the soul of its need for material prosperity with purpose."

— Suman Saran Sinha

"We are told to work for the sake of working, to earn for the sake of consuming, but without the grounding force of Dharma, Artha becomes a hollow pursuit that drains the life-force."

— Suman Saran Sinha

About the Author

Suman Saran Sinha has spent over four decades exploring the intersections of professional excellence, culture, and spirituality. He has written and published dozens of articles on philosophy, trade, economy, management, and social issues across diverse platforms. A poet at heart, his spiritually inspired poems in English and Hindi are shared on his personal blogs.

Suman's career spans law, management consulting, and corporate leadership. He has practiced as an Attorney before the High Court of Mumbai and the Supreme Court of India, served as Director and CEO across India, Russia, Canada, and the USA, and provided strategic consulting to international clients as a member of the Canadian Management Consulting Association (CMCA).

A committed educator and community leader, he has taught Yoga to numerous students in Toronto and held leadership roles in Rotary, business associations, and Indo-Russian cultural and business foundations. His experiences in professional, social, and spiritual spheres deeply inform his writing, which explores topics from Ancient Indian Civilization to reflections on etiquette, Samskara, hypocrisy, thinking, talking, obsession and many more.

A Note from the Author

Thank you for taking the time to journey through *Philosophy of Depression and Kriya Yoga – Investigating the Silence, Honouring the Struggle, Finding the Light.*

This book was written as an exploration of depression not merely as a psychological condition, but as a profound human experience that invites deeper inquiry into loneliness, meaning, consciousness, and spiritual transformation. If these pages have encouraged you to look beyond suffering and discover new possibilities for self-understanding, then their purpose has been fulfilled.

The ideas presented in this work did not emerge in isolation. They form part of a broader philosophical exploration developed over many years through observation, professional experience, study, reflection, and yogic practice.

Readers interested in exploring related themes may also find value in my other works

Philosophy of Loneliness (eBook)
An inquiry into the nature of loneliness, isolation, belonging, and the search for human connection in an increasingly fragmented world.

Philosophy of Yoga – Bhakti, Jnana and Karma Yoga in the Modern World and the Inner Kurukshetra
A contemporary exploration of Yoga as a philosophy of living, examining devotion, knowledge, selfless action, and the psychological battlefield that every individual faces within.

Together, these works explore different dimensions of a common question:

How does one live a meaningful, balanced, and awakened life in the modern world?

If this book has resonated with you, I encourage you to continue the journey—not by seeking answers from others, but by cultivating the courage to investigate your own experience with honesty, awareness, and compassion.

May your struggles become understanding.

May your understanding become wisdom.

May your wisdom become light.

With gratitude,

— *Suman Saran Sinha*

"Investigate the silence.
Honour the struggle.
Trust the journey.
The light was never at the end of the path—
it was the one who walked it."

Suggested Reading & Reference Sources

The ideas, interpretations, analogies, and philosophical frameworks presented in this book are the original reflections of the author, developed through decades of study, observation, professional experience, and spiritual practice. Classical scriptures, historical traditions, and publicly available educational resources have informed the broader context of the work. Readers interested in further exploration may consult:

- Patanjali's Yoga Sutras
- Bhagavad Gita
- Upanishads
- Teachings of Paramhansa Swami Satyananda Saraswati
- Publications of Bihar School of Yoga
- Literature on Kriya Yoga and Raja Yoga
- Contemporary literature on psychology, resilience, depression, mindfulness, and consciousness studies
- Resources published by recognized mental health organizations and professional psychological associations

Links for exploring my other works

- **Philosophy of Loneliness** - https://www.amazon.com/Philosophy-Loneliness-Suman-Saran-Sinha
- **Philosophy of Yoga** - Bhakti, Jnana, Karma in the Modern World – https://www.amazon.in/dp/9374260255

www.ingramcontent.com/pod-product-compliance
Lightning Source LLC
LaVergne TN
LVHW051932051126
851857LV00020B/2074
* 9 7 8 9 3 7 4 2 6 2 1 3 9 *